A RURAL MISCELLANY

A Rural
Miscellany

by
Roscoe Howells

ISBN: 0-84527-063-0

Cover design: Sian Parri

First published in 2006 by
Gwasg Carreg Gwalch, 12 Iard yr Orsaf, Llanrwst, Wales LL26 0EH
✆ 01492 642031   🖷 01492 641502
✆ books@carreg-gwalch.co.uk   Internet: www.carreg-gwalch.co.uk

**To the memory of those who shared and rejoiced
in so many of these offerings.**

*With thanks as ever to the splendid staff at Pembrokeshire
Records Office for their never failing help.*

Foreword

Provocative, prophetic and at times unashamedly passionate, this collection of articles penned by Roscoe Howells is rewarding in so many ways.

Provocative, as the reader will find, because the author uses his pen with vigour tempered by humour to bring errant officialdom into line, and with venom when a particular piece of bureaucratic nonsense made life more difficult for those who 'till the soil and tend the stock'. Roscoe Howells, as many will testify, was and is a good man to have on one's side.

Having himself as a farmer fallen victim to brucellosis, Roscoe's recovery was driven by his determination to convince the State that measures then being taken to rid the nation's herds of this debilitating disease were in need of drastic revision. That was just one of many battles in which he became engaged as a crusading columnist through his weekly Ben Brock column in *Welsh Farm News* and through articles for the *Western Telegraph* and other publications.

Prophetic because re-reading articles written more than thirty years ago, we realise that he outlined the scenario of global warming long before that became a fashionable pursuit for discussion. He was equally convinced that farming policy would become driven by environmental concerns rather than the provision of food for the nation's larder.

Passionate, in his love for the countryside and its ways, and especially in his deep affection for the well-being of the islands that lie off the Pembrokeshire coast.

I was one of a number of Roscoe's colleagues who shared in those days the largely rewarding task of recording the everyday affairs of farming in Wales, and beyond, in the 60s and 70s, and we all envied his ability to produce columns that were both informative and fun to read.

Whether it was attending a gathering of farmers, reporting a summer show, or visiting the big, bad city of London to report on the Dairy and Smithfield shows that once-upon-a-time brought an invasion of brown boots to the streets of the Capital, Roscoe invariably captured the lighter side of life. As he did in offbeat pieces relating a young city couple's experiences viewing a primitive country cottage, his personal quest for a slice of toast for breakfast while on a Butlin's holiday, and experience of hotels as he 'hithered and thithered' on various journalistic missions.

This miscellany reprises stories penned with earthy elegance enriched by his knack of recapturing the homespun humour that is part of the fabric of rural life.

But he could on occasion be seriously philosophical in columns written at Christmas which he found that much more meaningful with Jesus having been born in the manger of a stable because officialdom, in the form of a census, meant no room at the inn for Joseph and Mary.

For those who were not around or even born when many of Roscoe's articles first appeared, his echoes of times past will serve a dual purpose. Yes, it is history, but without the dust. By studiously avoiding the temptation to revise the original, the pieces remain as fresh as on the day or the night when they were written.

As the testimony of an eye witness of events at the time, this miscellany can be read as a matter of record, but laced with humour and, as Roscoe wrote when signing off many of his later contributions, 'so there 'tis then'.

David Lloyd, MBE, FRAgS, FGAJ and fellow scribe

A poor thing, sir, but mine own

As I recall it was upon this fashion. Just over fifty years ago, in May 1954, I called on the late H.G. Walters, at that time proprietor and editor of the old *Weekly News*, affectionately remembered as the *Narberth Paper*. I knew him well, and I said to him, 'I've been thinking about you.' 'Oh, aye,' he said, 'what have you been thinking?' I said, 'I've been thinking that here you are, making your living in a rural area, and you hardly ever mention farming, except occasionally in your own leading article, and then it's usually a heap of nonsense.' So he said, 'And what d'you reckon I ought to do about it?' And I said, 'Let me write a column for you.' That was how it all began. And he paid me, too. Not much, but he paid me.

It was a column called 'Countryside Commentary' under the pen-name Barn Owl, and it ran for three years. The first piece was about myxomatosis, the rabbit disease that had just hit Pembrokeshire. Then, in 1957, a weekly paper, *Welsh Farm News*, was launched. The late Sylvan Howells, the Public Relations Officer for the NFU in Wales, was asked whether he could recommend anybody, either a journalist who knew something about farming, or a farmer who could write, to cover south Wales.

It was a full-time commitment and, in addition to writing many farm features and reports, I was to write a weekly column called 'About The Farm', under the pen-name Ben Brock. I missed only one week, through sickness, until the paper folded twelve years later. Like the Barn Owl column, Ben Brock soon began to cover any and every subject that took my fancy.

Mixing, as I did, whilst working for the paper, with those from other papers and magazines, I was

8

sometimes asked to do a piece for them, and a few of such contributions are also included – a few, in Pembrokeshire, being any number more than about six, whilst a couple is no more than about three.

As time went by various people said that I am obviously an admirer of some character Damon Runyon, and in fact I never heard tell of this character until then, and now I discover that in fact he read some of the pieces I wrote in a former existence when I helped certain scribes to put together some of the stories they wrote in another collection which they call the Old Testament, and they are very ancient characters whatever.

For what it may be worth, for better or worse, richer or poorer, here is the collection, and may God bless all who sail in her.

Roscoe Howells

Welsh Farm News, 21 June 1958

It amuses me to read the would-be wise commentaries on local government affairs by people who would like you to believe they understand these things. With the local elections now over they write upon the status and composition of the County and District or Borough Councils. They sum it all up, and they really think they know.

Truth to tell, they haven't a clue.

For the real intrigue and cloak and dagger stuff, give me the Parish Council any day. Downing Street knows nothing compared with the plotting of the parish pump.

We nearly had an incident again this time.

To all intents and purposes it was just any ordinary post-meeting sort of night in the local. Jack-the-Pint was holding forth from the corner over the top of a glass big enough for him to fall in and drown. The other chaps knew a bit about this and that, but he was the only one who knew it all.

'It's all right,' says he, 'this Council lot always vote together. It doesn't matter if it's to shoot the Chairman as long as they all put their hands up together.'

Then he wanted to know about the starlings. He'd read in a paper that 2,500 starlings in 2½ hours could pick up how many hundredweights of corn.

'That's easy,' chimed in Jack Llew, 'they can agree and get on with it. If you was a starling you'd start a damn argument, and there'd be no corn picked all day.' With this devastating bit of repartee came drinks all round, and the Clerk to the Council, who is a fly sort of bird, was seen to be looking pretty well pleased with life and nobody knew why.

Now Jack-the-Pint wanted to know what about a bus shelter, and the Chairman said the only ones he ever saw going to catch a bus were out of breath from running and not hanging about waiting.

Even a worm can turn, however, and after getting this sort of answer all night, by the time it came to shut-tap Pint was all steamed up. Out came the Clerk with a nomination form and Pint, with a shaking hand, signed his name. The rest filled in the details. Trust them.

In the cold light of day the awful implications were brought home. Out of eleven sitting members only six had bothered to fill in a nomination paper. The other five reckoned on getting themselves deemed re-elected by default, or whatever long words it was the Clerk had been using.

With Pint now in the field and properly nominated – sponsored by the Chairman indeed – somebody would have to drop out.

There were now two schools of thought. Some reckon there was somebody the Clerk wanted to get rid of, but those in the know said it was between Pint and the Chairman, Davy Big-House. Davy Big-House had been bulldozing a bank to seed it and reclaim it. Pint reckoned it was only to get the subsidy. Obviously Pint was spoiling for a fight.

The upshot was, however, that they had turned out a gaggle of rats who upped and off into Pint's garden. That was Pint's story anyway. He did a day's work once and has never quite recovered from it. So what about his garden and how much compensation would there be because of the rats that were now bothering him? There was a law that said a man must keep his own stock on his own farm. Jack Llew wanted to know was it the rats had been at Pint's hedge.

There was no knowing where it might all have ended. Pint was on the spot. If he found himself on the Council with the Chairman's backing he'd have to shut up about the rats and maybe give him a couple of days at the hay as well.

Possibly he couldn't face up to that for, even at the risk of the others calling him cowardy custard, he wrote a very civil letter to the returning officer saying thank you very much all the same but not to bother.

He's finding it tough at the moment. The best he can think of as yet is to say that he was under the influence at the time of signing. He must have been. 'Them that's drunk at night,' says he, 'can always come sober. But them that's daft can never come wise.'

I'll admit he has a point there. And I reckon if he plays his cards right he'll be able to save face yet. But with all the intrigue that's going on it's a job to know. That's the point about intrigue. You just don't know where you are.

With County and District Councils it's obvious. They're fools and everybody knows it, so there we are. But the Parish Councils are different. They're a tough crowd. They're deep.

Even those on the inside have a job to know what's going on.

Welsh Farm News, 20 December 1958

I was telling you a while back you may remember about the near crisis with the Parish Council when everybody got three-sheets-in-the-wind just before election time and nominated Jack-the-Pint as prospective parish councillor. Pint, you will recall, withdrew in time with the profound observation that 'Them as is drunk at night can come sober, but them as is daft can never come wise'.

There was also the affair, which had precipitated all this, of the Chairman of the Council driving his rats into Pint's garden and so on and so forth. Things for a time looked black. Pint's stock went down considerably, and his position as ratepayers' advocate was in the balance for two successive Saturday nights when it was realised he'd been outmanoeuvred. With the advent of Christmas I am more than happy to report that there is nothing to report. All seems to have been forgiven. All is peace.

December's meeting of the brains of the parish consummated the seasonal alliance of the electors and the elected. Truth to tell, the meeting did not materialise. The Clerk arrived late but in time to light the fire.

The Chairman was next, twenty minutes afterwards, and then came the only other two destined to put in an appearance that night. By a process of elimination it was finally established that, of the remainder, one had 'flu, two were feathering, one had killed his pig, two had gone to some whist drive, one had to take his missus to be charmed for something or other, and the eighth only came once every six months anyway and would hardly choose the December meeting to be awkward.

The Clerk, who as I told you before, is a smug sort

of merchant, pointed out that this didn't constitute a quorum, so the Chairman wanted to know did he now have to give notion of motion or what was the procedure? The other two said as far as they were concerned it merely meant they could go and have a quick one, on which same there was entire and unanimous agreement.

All four consequently arrived at the pub before they were expected. They found that their two absent colleagues had finished feathering and were all present and correct. They had thought they would be too late for the meeting, and if they'd only known they would have come, and what d'you think of that? Even at this early hour Jack-the-Pint had had enough.

Back on his favourite subject, and with all the old bravado and knowledge, he wanted to know what the Parish Council had been up to. Bert the Stump, who lost a leg in an accident which must be told of some other day, and who hasn't missed a meeting of the Council for forty years, rose to the occasion in a statesmanlike and fitting manner befitting one of such hard-bitten parochial service.

It had been decided, he said, for the Parish Council to organise a carol-singing tour. Pint immediately wanted to know how this would affect the rates. Jack Llew offered the opinion that as they would drink the takings it would neither help the rates nor hinder them. He enlarged upon this to the extent of suggesting that if people had any sense they wouldn't give 'em enough to quench their thirst let alone get pickled.

This was sufficient to get Pint on his feet with an off-key rendering of that great old favourite, 'Why did I ever get married!' If you really don't know it, a postcard will be sufficient to secure the words. Llew said afterwards it sounded like a man wearing tack-boots trying to climb out of a corrugated iron tank and keeping on slipping back. This and the seasonal spirit were sufficient to entice the Clerk into a thunderous rendering of 'Thora'. Before the evening finally drew to an uncertain close they had forgotten about carol singing, the rates and elections. It is understood that these items will come up for fuller and more detailed consideration in the New Year.

Welsh Farm News, 27 June 1959

I am on holiday and, contrary to expectations, am having the time of my life.

You will remember, I hope, that oft times it has been my wont to retire west on such occasions to the island of Skomer, there to seek peace and solitude, and respite from the world's mad bustle and busy strife. But those days are gone, never to return.

You will know from your newspapers and television and wireless sets that you yourselves, the great British taxpayers, have bought the island for it to be established as a Nature Reserve. To this end the Nature Conservancy are possibly doing something useful, but there are facets about which so many of us who know Skomer well and love it dearly are not entirely happy.

It can only be assumed that what is being done is with the blessing of the N.C. Certainly statements have been made that this is so.

So this year I settled for a holiday as near the island as possible, with the intention of going for the day as often as circumstances would permit. And resigned, at the same time, to be miserable in the doing of it.

The writing is on the wall. But, brother, it has some compensations. Not least of which is one big belly laugh a dozen times a day. And this is where you and this column come into it for there is something going on round here that is going to revolutionise sheep-farming and livestock breeding as we know it.

One of the first moves was to put on the island about fifty little Soay ewes. Ever seen them? Like goats. Especially when you're in pursuit, which you most certainly are once they set eyes on you. Next we hailed the arrival of a hundred and twenty Welsh mountain ewes, eighty wethers ditto and three Kerry Hill rams.

With the run of 700 acres maybe you'd say that was

a good commercial proposition. I'd say you were right at that. The wethers to go off fat in the spring, and the Kerry Hill rams on the Welsh ewes to produce some useful lambs. We all figured they ought to show a fair profit. Especially if the grazing rights weren't too dear.

Which just goes to show you how misled you can be. When questions were asked about this lark it was explained that it was an experiment to cross the Welsh mountain sheep and the Soays. No one has yet let on as to how the Welsh ewes or wethers will mate with the Soay ewes. Nor is there news of Dr John Hammond being called in as yet.

But all in good time. Meanwhile one wag has written to a local paper suggesting that the Nature Conservancy might help things along by getting the Kerry Hill rams reclassified as a Welsh mountain breed.

The nearest I've heard tell of in this line previously was the bloke who tried crossing a kangaroo with Glamorgan sheep to get woollen jumpers. I reckon he'd get 'em and all. But not as good as if he'd put the kangaroo amongst that lot on Skomer. In fact the kangaroo would probably need a whole season's training on gulls' eggs before he'd catch 'em. The local fishermen, who also study form, figure that the Soays can leave the Welsh ewes by twenty yards and two stone walls in every fifty without bothering to put their ears back, and with the Kerry Hills nowhere.

To take charge of this little circus came a New Zealander who was introduced as a man of 'enthusiasm and toughness'. When he'd been there three weeks a parcel arrived and he thought, 'Ah, food at last!' But he was wrong again. It was a parcel of books. By this time his enthusiasm was definitely on the wane. Nor was he tough enough to eat the books.

If the local fishermen had not been keeping a humanitarian eye on him during this period he'd have been too weak to chew jellyfish with the ribs taken out. Eventually one of them found him in acute pain, in which state he had been for three days with badly torn ligaments. So he decided that both his enthusiasm and his toughness were at a low ebb.

He also showed perspicacity and a proper appreciation of the situation and did what you and I would have done in the same circumstances – thumbed a lift to the mainland. He has since intimated that he won't be around much any more.

More recently there's been a big performance of laying the foundation stone for the new bungalow. As you will have the pleasure of paying for this you will be pleased to know that you are having something which will cost about twice as much as the figure for which the builder says he would have been willing to do up the old house. And it is so situated as to catch pretty well every gale that blows. At the ceremony everything went well. They didn't wear hats so they couldn't be blown off. And a gentleman with a beard was imported the day before and installed in the hut on the door of which the word 'Warden' has been painted in bold red letters. So everything is under control and all we're waiting for now is news of the first lambs. What the hell they'll look like is anybody's guess.

All I know is that the moustachioed Secretary to the outfit, one of the newcomers to the bandwagon, was on the way over when a covey of puffins flew across the bow and he said, 'I say. Look at that. Are they ducks or geese?'

At any rate he was willing to ask.

Which I always say is a good thing in a world where there's so much to learn. Just look at what you lot didn't know about sheep-breeding, and you don't know the half of it.

Welsh Farm News, 24 September 1959

I am thinking it's a very good plan to get away from it all and it is one of the things on which I am definitely not one of the 'don't knows'.

You can think I've gone round the bend at last if you wish, but I'll tell you where I'm going, and that's over the waves to Skomer.

You will know that things aren't what they were out there because I wrote about it last June. And you can't stay out there now. The good old days are gone.

Signposts have been erected so that visiting suburbia can see for themselves, 'Bird's nest this way – eggs laid by here'. Planning permission for an ice cream kiosk is expected to be announced daily.

The sheep experiment was very suddenly abandoned. The locals reckoned that too many of the ewes were suspected of belonging to the 'don't knows'.

It is, however, rumoured that the Min. of Ag. and Fish. (and Food) have been persuaded to persuade the Nature Conservancy to forbid the catching of rabbits so that it does not encourage bad habits on the mainland where they can't catch them either, because they don't know how to. The idea seems to be to try to poison them and call it scientific research, even if it involves killing the little Skomer voles which are found nowhere else in the world. This is because it is a reserve for wildlife as you will have read in the papers.

First of all, however, they are trying to get a grant to compensate them for the loss in revenue they will sustain by not having the money they would otherwise receive if they were not wanting the rabbits not to be caught. When this grant has been obtained scientific research can begin, so thanks from one and all, to you as taxpayers, for all your help. This is known as wanting not only the penny and the bun, but jam on it as well.

But there is a chance of this one last, long farewell. The bungalow on which you, as taxpayers, have wasted your money, is nearing completion and the good men and true who have stuck so nobly to the task of building it are always glad of a volunteer helper, provided it's a civil sort of badger and very friendly like I am when people aren't upsetting me by putting on the clock and holding elections and such nonsense. Word cometh that next week they'd be glad of an experienced tea-maker, dabber-on-of-paint and odd-job factotum. I'm a useful sort of badger at that. Very handy.

By the time this appears in print it will be too late for anybody to ask questions concerning qualifications as such or whether I possess a union card to perform said duties. The rest of you can carry out the inquest on why the 'don't knows' did know and what they knew. And how they knew.

I'm just going, mate, that's all.

I'll be beyond the reach of telephone, postman, newspaper and humanity in general. And blow the wind never so coldly, if you can find a place like that, mate, it's a very good place to be.

Welsh Farm News, 31 October 1959

When I took my leave for what I, at any rate, am convinced was a well-earned holiday, I thought that maybe you could manage for a week or so without my erudite observations on matters agricultural. The thought occurs, however, that rather than see a blank in the usual corner, and matters agricultural being out of the question at the moment, you might, in lieu of, like to know how things are shaping on this fair island. For if you read last week's edition you will remember that I was bound for Skomer.

Dark and stormy waters delayed the crossing for twenty-four hours, but now I'm here. And there's an outside chance that arrangements might be made for these lines to reach the Editor's desk so that you will be able to keep yourselves up-to-date. And believe me, friends, you have a finger in this pie. Whether you like it or not. But we'll come to that bit later.

First of all I should tell you that, on arrival, I discovered that those who might now be regarded as residents and who have reverted to something little better than half savage, had refused to put the clock back. Rather like the artistic type who handed in his day return ticket at the barrier and, on having it pointed out to him that it was nearly a year out-dated, explained to the inspector that time mattered not to him.

So then, with these people. And, in view of my never-ending campaign against this iniquity, that probably makes you laugh your eye out. But it does serve to emphasise the sense of leaving the thing alone all the year round.

It merely means that unlike the sailor who got up with the lark and went to bed with the wren, we get up with the lark and go to bed with the gulls. In between times everything else is an hour earlier than with the rest of the country. We are occasionally reminded of this because, in the way the old-time traders undermined the way of life of the Red Indians, some rotten white man flogged a portable radio to these poor innocents. Such is the extent of our depravity.

When this miserable box is not churning out the worst that Radio Luxembourg can offer, it is switched on to the news and then immediately turned off because nobody wants to be that miserable. So that, for the most part, it's a case of forgotten by the world and by the world forgot.

But I wouldn't like you to forget the wonderful bungalow which you taxpayers, via the Nature Conservancy, have almost finished building here. It sure is some shack, friends. It was so important to stick it in the right place that, in order to counteract the fearful slope, sufficient concrete blocks went into the foundation to build a cavity-walled bungalow of the same size on any flat part of the island. When you realise that there are at least 400 acres of dead flat land on which to build you will see how important it was to have it where it is.

These blocks were imported after the fearful row which followed exposure of the fact that the foundations were supposed to be of the stones which would have to be torn from the old farm walls where the Manx shearwaters make their nests.

In this three-bedroomed bungalow there are kitchen sinks various, one bath and three WCs. So that there shall be no room for doubt let me explain that this abbreviation stands for water closet. And there are three of them.

The fact that the joint has been stuck near the well which, in anything like a dry season, won't provide enough water to keep even one of the closets going is the concern and misfortune of those who won't be able to use them.

Light is to be provided by liquid gas with a patent name. In addition to two geysers and one cooker there are to be no fewer than 34 (thirty-four) lights! There are other items, friends. But don't let me bore you.

Small wonder that you taxpayers are now running out of cash and it has been decreed, for example, that you can't afford a decent grate for the lounge. Instead you have had to settle for a ye olde worlde effort made of pebbles from the beach. Odds and ends of items that would cost another copper or two are strictly taboo. The economy drive is on. So rejoice ye taxpayers and be of glad heart.

As to the future, there are already signs that the Skomer voles are in for a high old time tearing up the insulation board which lines this wonderful cedar-wood bungalow. But you taxpayers refused to settle for spending half as much money to do up the old farmhouse. Stones and slates weren't good enough. So on your own heads be it.

By candle light conference the other night we decided that if you could see the head boss struggling to get a tractor up a gradient of 1 in 3 you'd decide he was crackers. He said he decided he was crackers long ago after he could see what he had taken on by coming here at all.

Last time I was hereabouts I wrote a little piece for you about the experiment of crossing Welsh Mountain ewes with Soay ewes. You might as well call the latter goats and be done with. You'd be much nearer the mark.

I think I explained to you last week that the experiment has already been accounted a failure. The Welsh Mountain ewes have all been recaptured and removed. All bar one. She, poor lonely soul, is still chasing the Soays round the rocky perimeter of this 700-acre stronghold.

After the drought and shortage of grass you can take my word for it that she is now in superb racing condition. And then some. Maybe I'll open a book so that my most excellent companions can state their case as to what they think might happen if she ever does catch up with them.

Maybe they're all just dashing for the blade of grass they thought they saw about to grow. For everything is now so bare that one evening a rabbit was seen on top of a clump of brambles where he had climbed in search of some green leaf. One of my old masters at school used to say that a phenomenen was a cow sitting on a thistle. He just didn't know a thing, and his false teeth were loose, anyway, so we were inclined to laugh.

You will know from all this that I am well-content with my humble portion here below. I lack for nothing. I don't even have to open my own tins as in days of yore.

In preparation for this screed I said to the most estimable, blue-eyed colleen, a true daughter of owld Oireland, who ministers to our every need, 'And what shall I be after sayin' about you, my darlint?'

To which she replied, 'Say not'in' at all as long as it's the trut'.'

Yes indeed. 'Say nothing at all as long as it's the truth.' Not a bad motto I'm after thinking. And, so help me, every word of what I've written is true enough.

It also explains about the Irish.

And so, to the strains of Tommy Steele shouting his guts out on Radio Luxembourg, I bid you good-day. I'll be back bye and bye. Worst luck.

Welsh Farm News, 7 November 1959

It made a big story in the national press, and caused great amusement amongst farming people, when newcomers to the rural life, who reckon to know all about it if they own three acres and a hen, were outraged when the Ayrshire bull, which they had bought as a calf and then reared as a pet, was turned down by the Ministry's Livestock Officer as being unsuitable for breeding purposes.

Ode on the affair of the beautiful bull condemned to
    a fate worse than death:
The tale which now I must relate,
    is of a bull whose cruel fate
Decreed that he should have no mate,
    but lead a life most celibate.
For when he came to man's estate,
    there came from some Inspectorate
A man who did in name of State,
    demand precaution ultimate.
This creature most effeminate,
    which had an air so delicate,
Must never ever perpetrate,
    the act of being profligate.
No wedding bells to celebrate,
    no wedded bliss to contemplate,
No marriage should he consummate,
    no nasal ring to show his state.
The farmer now could nominate,
    the service of a bull sedate
And all his cows inseminate,
    from test-tubes most elaborate.
Let no one now expostulate,
    or with inspectors remonstrate.
His beauty did not palliate,
    nor noble breeding mitigate.

No matter if they titivate,
   his horns with blossoms roseate
And feed him strawberries on a plate,
   sweetness does not extenuate.
They said they would not contemplate,
   to license him to propagate
Poor progeny most delicate,
   and call him 'Papa', any rate.
Indeed they could not tolerate,
   the thought that he'd disseminate
Such offspring very underweight,
   and they remained most obdurate.
Such things they must eradicate,
   with zeal and fervour passionate,
No matter who should agitate,
   these faults they must exterminate.
They put the order on the slate,
   decreeing by a given date
That either they must operate,
   or make him meat upon a plate.
And whether it were soon or late,
   this would have been his painless fate,
But someone did with pincers great,
   confer on him a doctorate.
Essential parts to extricate,
   was just a simple task quite straight,
Referred to since an early date,
   by good old-fashioned word, castrate.
To give the wrong idea we'd hate,
   this bull they did emasculate.
That's all there really is to state,
   and now this tale we terminate.

Whilst Ferdinand can rue his fate,
   and meanwhile sadly meditate
Why fools their folly demonstrate,

and worse than death must be his fate.
And as we turn to sterner stuff,
    forgetting all about this guff,
Just spare a thought as faces redden –
    I'm sorry for the bloke who bred'n.

Welsh Farm News, 25 June 1960

The other evening on the old goggle-box on that well-known programme 'Tonight' there appeared one small pig.

Having appeared on this programme a couple of times myself I am prepared to say that, yes, they do rake up some oddities on it occasionally. Even so, I didn't quite get round to the idea of why they had to have the small pig on the programme.

It seems that the lady, who had it on a lead, was rather fond of it, that they were rearing it on a well-known baby food, and that she did hope so much that when it grew up to be a real proper big pig that it wouldn't turn out to be a bore.

That's what I thought she said anyway.

And I do so hope she's right. Otherwise we might find ourselves with another Ferdinand on our hands, which would be such a shame, especially when this little pig is so very clever and always lets them know when he wants to go outside.

Which just goes to show you, doesn't it? For *à propos* nothing in particular I found myself calling to mind those immortal lines from a Frank Crumit song:

'Twas a night in late October
When I was one third sober
I was taking home a load with manly pride,
My poor feet began to stutter
And I lay down in the gutter
And a pig came up and lay down by my side.
We sang a song fair weather,
Like all good pals together,
When a lady passing by was heard to say
'You can tell a man who boozes
By the company he chooses',

And the pig got up and slowly walked away.

Such intelligent creatures, don't you think?

Welsh Farm News, 23 July 1960

You may have read a number of reports recently about sheep being killed by lightning on St Margaret's Island off the coast of Pembrokeshire.

They are the Soay sheep about which I write a couple of pieces for you last year as a result of a plan which is passed off as an alleged experiment to cross Welsh Mountain ewes with Soay ewes on Skomer Island. And I tell you as much as I think will be helpful to you about these Soays and how fast they can run and how they can jump.

So you know something about Soays. In this particular case they are on this St Margaret's Island which is about eighteen acres and there are about thirty of them. Now I take it that after all the articles by NAAS and one and all in this paper generally about rates of stocking and all the rest of it, that you will agree that thirty sheep on eighteen acres will be getting a bit tired of life generally after about ten years.

In a season like last summer you can imagine what it must be like for these poor sheep without any grass or any water. So a young lady writes to the head boss who put them there and says she is very worried about these sheep as local boatmen tell her that a number of them have died. But nothing is done.

Then, in the winter, somebody writes in to say they have all died and there is a big furore. A vet goes over and says there isn't enough grass to keep two sheep in March, even after the thirty sheep have all been dead since December. And they know they have been dead since December because the man in charge says they are obviously struck by lightning.

Then they all go up to Aberystwyth and have a big meeting with some for and some against.

The organisation's chief says the poor little Soay

sheep were not hungry because they could have eaten seaweed like some sheep he once reads about used to do two thousand years ago, but nobody knows that the sheep would have been too weak to get down to the seaweed, and how would you like to try eating it?

Then a lady who is a great animal lover and who thinks it is a grand idea to leave thirty ewes for months on end on a bare eighteen-acre rock without food or water gets up and says she knows about farming, and she knows that sheep can be struck by lightning because she once sees a dead ewe floating down the river.

But I happen to know, and you also know as a result of all I previously write for you about all this malarkey, that this is all bunkum. Because it so happens, apart from anything else, that lightning could never catch up with these sheep because they are so quick.

Last week I have a week's holiday, and although I do not go to Skomer because I have not yet acclimatised myself to the idea of what is going on there, which I tell you about previously, there are other islands to be had.

And I think it is a very good idea to get away to a lonely island for a holiday to be away from people such as these characters, who make me lose my good opinion of the human race, so that I can contemplate all the wonders of Nature.

Especially lightning.

Welsh Farm News, 6 August 1960

I told you I was going on holiday, didn't I, and here I am. Though when or whether you will ever read this is anybody's guess and dependent on the weather and whether a boat ever passes this way.

For you know where I go when the spirit moves. It's over the waves to the islands. And this time it's Skokholm. Further out than Skomer and even less accessible.

But there are people here. Creatures of odd habits, I find, but they have their uses. They cook, for example, and help with the washing up, and everybody mucks in together and, taking it in turns we pump away to get water from the well to the tank, which is all frightfully jolly. In any case there's only a dozen of us, so the washing up and pumping doesn't really amount to very much.

There's also a lighthouse with three friendly keepers who are glad to see anybody from the outside world. Upon being asked why he became a lighthouse keeper, one said it was because he isn't right in the head. I don't believe this, however. They all seem quite all right to me. One is so browned off that he is just waiting for the day when he comes up on the Pools so that he can buy a lighthouse of his own. Which just goes to show you.

In between times, whilst we are not washing up and pumping water, we watch birds and that and everybody puts rings on their legs (the birds' legs) and they all make a lot of notes in books. I don't think you'd be very interested in this.

But there is one little point about which I feel I ought to tell you. It's about the Soay sheep. You'll die laughing. For you remember before I set off I told you about what happened to the thirty-odd Soay sheep on eighteen-acre St Margaret's Island that got struck by lightning before they could get down to eat the seaweed like they used to do two thousand years ago. Well, there were some Soays on Skokholm. About seventy or so. But although the island is over two hundred acres it was decided last autumn to get rid of them because it was so bare there would not be enough for them to last the winter. Especially if they couldn't get down to the seaweed! And they might not be struck by lightning the same as the ones on St Margaret's, which would very conveniently put them out of their suffering.

So everybody went out on a bateau and shot about sixty Soays, leaving a dozen. During the winter ten of these died, but I don't know why, and then there were two. These two are still here. And they are ewes. Which leads me to the point of the story.

When I wrote to you from Skomer last year about the experiment of crossing Welsh Mountain ewes with Soay ewes, I told you that these creatures looked more like goats. Certainly none of the other sheep ever met up with the Soays and they just wouldn't have any truck with them. But out here it's different. For we have some goats. They don't belong to anybody, but they're here.

They don't belong to the lighthouse anyway. And they don't belong to us. But it seems they were left here by 'the bird people' sometime.

Once upon a time there was a billy goat and there was a nanny.

This island is three miles from land and it is very pleasant here. I should imagine, though, that time could hang very heavy on your hands, especially in winter, if you were such a silly old goat that you didn't have much interest in birds, and when the birds have all gone away.

So now there is also a young goat here and that makes three. As luck would have it he's a young billy. And that's going to complicate things. But as I was saying about these Soays. I said before that they looked like goats. And the proof of the sheep is in the mating. I'm not sticking my neck out. Not saying anything at all. I'm just lying on the cliff catching up on some sleep to which I am very partial and now and again keeping an eye on the sheep and goats and things in general.

And the Soays and the goats have palled up. Yes, but definitely. Not yet living on what you might call intimate terms, but definitely something more than just good friends. They graze maybe ten yards apart.

But I know about goats. And I've seen this dirty great billy goat with a long beard, and a wicked look in his eye, and I'll wager I know what he's thinking. And my betting is that if the Soays aren't a good bit more careful than they're being at the moment they're going to miss the last 'bus home one dark night just when they're least expecting it.

Especially with the youngster beginning to sit up and take notice.

If ever that should happen I'd like to come out here again to report back. But there's a dead keen birdwatcher here who has just left school and is going to start going to college to learn to be a vet. He's going to spend six years learning to be a vet. I've spent all my life thinking about sheep and billy goats and the birds and the bees and that.

I have been propounding my views, and this boyo says that it won't happen and, even if it does, nothing will happen because of Jean's, and I said what the hell did Jean have to do with it? It's the dirty great Billy is the one to watch.

And you know, and I know, that I know what I'm talking about.

Welsh Farm News, 12 November 1960

Every day in every way the world is becoming more and more conscious of the fact that this is the day of the Public Relations Officer. Particularly is this so in the world of agricultural organisations, merchandise and what-have-you.

I thought maybe you would therefore like me to explain to you about P.R.O.'s. I can do this because, as you know, I can always explain about everything, which just shows how lucky you are.

When I am in London for the Dairy Show one of these P.R.O.'s decides it is time he gets to know some of the boys from the country a bit better, because he is becoming a bit sick of the sight of some of the London crowd anyway. So you will see straightaway that this boyo knows his onions and gets five star ranking from the word 'go'.

Before we start off for the appointed place we have just about the right amount to decide that the world is a good enough place in which to live. The underground is out of the question, because we have no time to waste observing framed adverts of female foundation garments looking like pudding basins.

Normally this will mean a taxi, but fortunately one of the number has a motor car handy and knows his way past the traffic lights, and is also fit to drive, for he is aware of his responsibilities, and is only mixing his straight tomato juices with an occasional dry ginger.

Obviously it is impossible to start the meal without an appetiser.

We have with us one of these great characters who should have been dead twenty years ago. When the doctors tell him he has to take it easy he decides life will not be worth living that way. So he starts to go the pace for one last fling to go out in style and since then he never looks back. Which surely goes to prove something.

There is an anxious-looking waiter now hovering in the background, and he whispers in the ear of the convenor of the meeting about the table now being ready. So the convenor says to the old chap: 'If we don't go now we'll lose our table, so shall we go and eat or have another drink and wait for another table?'

And the old chap says, 'That's a grand job. We'll have 'em both.'

Whilst this little drink is being enjoyed the head waiter comes along and says to the old chap, 'You see, sir, if you don't come and take your table now I'll have to let it go.'

'That's fine, boy,' says the old chap, 'you let it go.'

So the head waiter says, 'Yes, sir, but then we won't have a table for you.'

'That's damn silly talk' says the old chap, 'we've booked one.'

'Yes, sir' says the head waiter.

We have our little drink. And another little drink as far as I remember. And maybe one more. And then we have our little meal.

The old chap starts quietly with one dozen large oysters and I never expect to see such a sight again.

There are lots of gentlemen about with long white aprons and large white hats, and some of them are pushing a sort of trolley with spirit lamps or something, presumably to keep things warm, and there is half-a-ton of beef on top of it.

Then one of the gentlemen in a white hat comes along and slices off large lumps, and I never eat so much in all my life. I should also say that I do not have a mouthful since breakfast for I am a very busy badger all day. But by night we badgers really do come into our own.

I don't know if you ever notice how easy it is to lose track of time. Anyway, it must be very late when somebody tells a very funny story about a black man, but I can't remember why. Maybe he just wants to tell a funny story. We have also been joined by a famous cattle breeder and I don't think he stops laughing yet.

There is also a Scot, who by now has enough of his native beverage to be really miserable, and he is explaining about the problems of some people in the middle of Scotland where there are five million acres of heather and waste land, and it is very difficult to get a living there, so somebody says they ought to form their own farmers' union or something, or have a law against it.

He is so upset about all this, in fact, that we decide to take him for a drink to cheer him up a bit. But when we get to this club place to have a little drink the Scot is missing, and it looks as if he calls it a day. So I decide to have the odd one for him, just to be sociable, and then take a leaf out of his book and drift.

But first of all the old chap listens patiently to the steward of the club who says his little piece very nicely about the rules of the club, and then the old chap explains that he always believes in making his own rules anyway and the steward says 'Yes, sir.'

When we come out, the starlings or sparrows or whatever it is, are kicking up hell's delight in the darkness above, and it's a wonder the Londoners don't form some eradication societies.

Fortunately the boyo on the tomato juice, who is incidentally the convenor of the meeting, is still in the offing and he drops us off near the bright lights where all the pretty popsies lark about until Lord Wolfenden stops their nonsense. It is far too late to go down amongst the pudding basins, so all you do in such circumstances is walk right out into the middle of the traffic, hold up your hand and say 'Taxi' – and it works. When this kind soul has deposited me safely outside my humble lodgings I repair to an all-night joint I know of and drink three or four pints of milk straight, which is a good thing to do.

At 6.00 a.m. I don't know whether my name is Ben Brock or if it is Thursday, so I rise from my revolving bed and plunge my fevered brow and throbbing head into a wash-basinful of cold water, resolved once more to remain a teetotaller for ever.

This explains about P.R.O.'s and the great service they perform in converting everybody into becoming teetotallers.

Welsh Farm News, 24 December 1960

They say that as you grow older the years go by more quickly, and certainly I find it hard to believe that once again the time is here to be writing my Christmas column.

There are times when I find this weekly effort a bit of a bind but, for the most part, I can honestly say I quite enjoy it.

However humdrum it might be, like life itself, I have always thought that at Christmas time at any rate it is no bad plan to pause awhile and see what it's all about. And this is something which most of us recognise every Christmas as something we do all too infrequently.

This year, for the first time in my life, I shall be spending Christmas away from home. So you will see that I have had a great deal for which to be thankful over the years.

This year, however, sickness has struck and things will not follow the more accepted pattern.

Some of you sometimes ask me whether there is a Mrs Brock. And this is an odd question, because no-one could possibly go on writing a column such as this without a power behind the throne, to inspire when thought is blank, to encourage when despondency prevails and, not least, to censor, wisely but ever so firmly, when the vitriol runs too freely.

When a loved one on whom you rely for these things is suddenly removed from the scene you are very much aware of your own shortcomings and inadequacy. And you write a column which, looking over your shoulder if only she could be there to do so, she would tell you to throw in the waste-paper basket.

Even though they like to be appreciated they don't want you to be telling the world about it. So maybe I'll get a bit of a rattling when she comes home and I don't mind telling you I'll be thankful for it. For who would have thought that a house could be so dead and miserably silent?

For, as I told you, sickness has struck and Mrs Brock is in hospital. Yet the news is that, with anything like luck, she should be out for Christmas. And as she is in a Manchester nursing home it means that she will spend Christmas in Lancashire. This has the consolation of being very acceptable to one small badger.

And off hand, I can't think of any people amongst whom I would prefer to be at such a time. Mind you, I don't want to be misunderstood. I am very happy to have been born in the Land of My Fathers and all that and to go on living in it. But if there are any more warm-hearted people on God's earth than the Lancastrians I've never met them.

It is, too, a source of wonderful comfort to find your friends. And I think I can say that there have been times when my faith in mankind has plumbed the depths when those believed to be friends have been seen in their true colours.

You will be able to understand, however, that a few weeks ago I was feeling pretty much down in the dumps about all this business generally. Then, when the operation was over and things looked perhaps less black, I set off for home on a miserable foggy morning.

At five minutes to eight I heard subconsciously on the car radio the weather forecast for the day. It was for more fog and floods and snow and ice patches and everything you didn't want all spreading from everywhere in all directions.

Then, just as if that wasn't enough to be going on with, they followed up with the news headlines – President de Gaulle was getting ready to go to Algiers and trouble was expected. Hostages in the Congo would have their heads cut off. Some civil servants were to get a £20-million salary increase. A youth had been stabbed to death in London. The police had issued a description of some poor half-crazed woman somewhere in England.

And, coming on top of everything else, perhaps I can be forgiven for wondering what it was all coming to.

Then, somewhere between Warrington and Chester, as the fog began to lift a little and daylight showed signs of returning, I passed through a village where there was rather a nice church with a lychgate. And on the lychgate was written in white lettering: 'I am the resurrection and the life.'

And things like this just turn up every now and again to remind us of the promise made to us. And we remember, all too casually, the many blessings for which we should give thanks.

Thus it is, as we turn in thought once again to Bethlehem, the Star, the Wise Men and the Christ Child, different thoughts, for different reasons, will come to many of us.

Amongst those we remember will be those in hospital, far away from their loved ones, and there will be those wonderful people who care for them.

For my own part, giving thanks for many things, I will be especially thankful for the skill and devotion of those who have helped to make incurable illnesses curable, and for a loved one safely delivered from dark shadows.

And, remembering the true message of this season, I can but offer you the wish that the Spirit of peace and goodwill may fill your hearts and abide with you throughout the coming year.

Welsh Farm News, 28 January 1961

Now it came to pass that there was great trouble in the land, wherefore the shepherds and humble men who tilled the soil were troubled and sore distressed. Nor was there money for them to do unto their land that which the law required of them to do. For there were wise men amongst the rulers of the people, who spake unto the shepherds and humble men of ferts and efficiency that they might grow the grass that was in the field to be green like unto an emerald.

Even so it was manifest to all men that ferts and the seed with which the sower must needs go forth to sow, and the machines to work in the fields with great noise, and even the beasts of the fields themselves, could only be had by the shepherds and humble men in return for many pieces of silver.

And when the shepherds and humble men required these things that they might do unto the land that which it was meet and right for them to do, yet had not the pieces of silver to render unto those that would sell them, they were sore troubled, and men would say of them they were like unto one who was up the creek, and sometimes even without a paddle, which was a saying that passeth all understanding, but was after the manner of speaking of these times.

Therefore would the shepherds and humble men go unto those who were known amongst men as bank managers. And these would be known as Rees, the Bank, or Evans, the Bank. And many of them again would be called Thomas or Jenkins or Davies, according to whosoever would have been his father, which sometimes the shepherds and humble men would say they could not be sure of, but always would it be of the Bank. And this was in order that they could be identified with the manner of their calling.

Now these men, who were known as bank managers, dwelt in great buildings with iron bars and mighty doors, which were also of iron, wherein they kept many bags full of pieces of silver, and they were as the young man who buried his talents in the ground. So would the shepherds and humble men go unto these bank mangers who sitteth with their backs to the window so that the light might fall upon the countenance of the shepherds and humble men, and the bank managers would be as those in the shadows that perceiveth all things.

And the bank manager would speak unto the humble man after this manner: How many beast of the field hast thou? And the humble man would look upon the floor and speak thiswise: I have bought my land, wherefore I have left to me no pieces of silver and but few beasts of the field, but doest thou lend me some pieces of silver that I might do unto my land that which it is meet and right for me to do, and I shall then repay thee an hundred fold. But if thou doest this not, then my land shall remain infertile and be choked with weeds and become like unto the desert.

But the bank manger would speak sadly and in manner showing great compassion, and he would say: Knowest thou not that it is written, To him that hath shall it be given, and from him that hath not it shall be taken away, even that little which he hath. Even so if these were mine own pieces of silver I would entrust them to thee as to mine own brother, but I have many masters who dwell in the cities, and they shall require that thou hast great possessions before they shall entrust thee with their pieces of silver.

Thus would the shepherds and humble men go unto the usurers and financiers, which was called the never-never, the manner whereof being simple to understand because there was never any hope of paying them back, so great was the interest they charged, and they never allowed the shepherds and humble men not to make their repayments, and rather would they take away from the shepherds and humble men the beasts of the field, and the machines to work with great noise, and sell them in the market place for as little as was still owing on them, and it was a yoke and burden most grievous and heavy to bear.

Yet these troublous conditions could not have come to pass were it not for the bank mangers who would not part with their pieces of silver.

So it was that men spake in parables of the bank managers saying wherefore the sun was shining they would offer to lend unto men a covering unto their heads, yet if sobeit the rain did fall so would they summon men to appear before them wherefore they might demand the return of the covering which would protect them from the rain.

So also did men say of a bank manger that he had a glass eye, and it was easy to perceive, for this was the eye which showeth most sympathy, wherefore would men laugh when this was said at places where they sat down to eat in large numbers annually, even though they had heard this being said many times before. And this was because the shepherds and humble men went in fear and trembling of their bank managers.

A *Rural Miscellany*

Welsh Farm News, 26 August 1961

I have just been looking at the Sunday papers with my
feet up on the mantelpiece and am minded to take a
little shut-eye which is a very pleasant way to pass the
afternoon even if it is not entirely healthy.

It is also surprising what evil and great foolishness
there is in the world which you will not wot of unless
you read the Sunday papers. And it is indeed
surprising that there is any evil left to write about when
you consider that every Sunday paper lifts the lid off at
least one pot of great wickedness each week.

But accustomed as we are to the public
demonstrations of great foolishness on which some
folks are hell-bent, as witness the odd bits in every
Sunday paper every week, I reckon the bit about the
grey squirrel and the RSPCA Inspector this week just
about takes the bun.

If we are to believe this story it seems that this here
grey squirrel is found as a youngster in poor shape and
reared by this here Inspector. The animal or rodent, or
whatever you call it, is reared on milk, to which it
becomes quite partial, and from which you will realise
that the squirrel is considerably brighter than the
Inspector, who then tries to release the thing into a
wood. Fortunately the squirrel isn't having any.
Naturally enough, not knowing quite what makes the
world go round or how many nuts make five, the
squirrel shows a decided disinclination for having to
leave a ready supply of milk and oatmeal biscuits.

I subscribe to the belief that it is quite wrong to rear
wild animals in captivity, partially domesticate them,
and then, when they have lost many of their natural
instincts of self-preservation, release them to await
their fate.

This Inspector says that he belongs to a humane

society and it his job to prevent the suffering of animals. Now it is a free country, and you can still think what you like about these things, including the RSPCA, and I think they are a shower.

Whilst acknowledging that certain flat-heeled, wool-stockinged females are frightfully sincere with their slotted tins and little flags on collecting days, the plain truth is that thinking people no longer take this bunch very seriously.

Having been turned out to the woods, the grey squirrel will be at the mercy of mankind by whom he is recognised as a considerable pest. There he will be, skulking about in the tree tops, when a gentleman with a gun who, even if he is wearing the right gaiters, might have a whitlow on his trigger finger, and instead of ringing down the curtain for the squirrel, succeeds only in shooting him right up the sky-rocket.

This will be a contingency most grievous and extremely painful for the poor little squirrel, who will leap away in great distress and six long jumps, to a place where he will die a lingering death in considerable torment. Much better for the little squirrel in fact if he is put out of his suffering in the first place.

In this particular case it would seem from the story in the Sunday paper that the Ministry of Agriculture are a little cross with the RSPCA Inspector because of his great foolishness in wanting to release the squirrel.

Much as it goes against the grain I agree with the Min. of Ag. Anybody with the interests of wild animals at heart, and this should include even those belonging to the RSPCA, must realise that man was created in his Maker's image with an intellect superior to that of the wild animals to whom he therefore has considerable responsibility.

It is a simple fact that in some cases we have to destroy wild animals to mould Nature to our own hand. And, as I no doubt say to you previously, I take as my authority for saying this the best book to which I can refer you, and to Genesis therein, Ch. 1, Verses 26-28.

And God said: 'Let us make man in our own image, after our likeness: and let them have dominion over the fish of the sea, and over the fowl of the air, and over all the earth, and over every creeping thing that creepeth upon the earth.'

Welsh Farm News, 11 November 1961

Maybe you will remember that about a year ago I write a little piece for you about P.R.O.'s in which I explain how it is they have the trick of being able to convert people into becoming teetotallers, and how it is that I become a teetotaller, or very nearly.

Well, this year when I am at the Dairy Show I meet up with the same character who says, 'Ben,' he says, 'I have something lined up for you' he says. And he also explains that he has some other odd bods he is very anxious for me to meet, and he tells me why. 'Furthermore,' he states, 'I will put you more stupid than you ever are in your life before.'

Personally I have some very serious doubts about this, what with knowing how stupid I am in my time, and also remembering that I am very nearly teetotal. But I do not see this as any cause for great argument and merely pass it off by saying, 'I will be very pleased to meet your friends.'

Now there is no great detail to fill in about how we get to this place as it is a most uneventful journey which is in no way cause for any excitement whatever. But once we are there, and all duly assembled, it is obvious that we are right ready to begin to commence, and ye festive spirit descends upon one and all.

Straightaway we are all conducted downstairs to a very nice dining room, but apart from that you will not recognise it, for it is not like anything you ever see before because it is definitely ye old worlde, and you must forget all about Kruschev, bank managers, milk quotas, the wet weather and anything else about which you feel you will like to forget.

The idea is that you now put the clock back about three hundred and fifty years, and you can imagine what this does to me, for it is well-known to one and all what I think about this mucking about with the clock for merely one hour twice a year.

This is now in the time of the first Elizabeth and there is only candlelight and some oak tables and no tablecloths. There is also some rush on the floor because slatted floors are not yet invented.

As soon as you sit down a very beautiful character who is wearing the sort of clothes appropriate to these times comes along and ties a big napkin, which is whiter than white, round your neck. But as soon as she speaks you know she is no ordinary serving wench, in fact she is real class.

But I will say no more on the subject in case I am misunderstood, except to state that she has what it takes and then some, and also a lot of this and that where it matters. Nor will I speak in great detail of the food, which is out of this world and in great quantity. It is also very different from other such high class eating establishments as you will find in this City where they always have many rows of cutlery stretching away in all directions to cause great confusion, and I always pick the wrong ones and end up looking very foolish.

At this place there are only two to last you right through the whole meal. One is a knife and the other is a bifurcated dagger. Or that is what they tell me it is called, but I am afraid that this might be a rude expression I never hear before and they are pulling my leg, so I just call them both the stabbers. But because of the nasty twist I have in my mind I must state that this strikes me as a big saving when it comes time to do the washing up.

I should also say that there is some drink about, which is mead and claret and ale, which is in very sensible sized drinking mugs because they are quite large.

There are also about fifty or sixty other characters,

male and female, in this very nice place, and every now and again, for no reason as far as I can see, one of them will get up and bang on the table with his mug and shout 'All hail'. Then everybody else will shout back 'Wassail', which is regarded as very civil in these times.

It is also a good excuse to get rid of some more of this mead and claret and stuff, but as one of these pleasant female characters who is all laced up here and there, is going round topping up all the empty mugs from a large jug, there is not much point in emptying them except to shout a lot of Wassails every now and again.

About this time the P.R.O. leans across to where I am sitting and tells me about his wife who is, or so he claims, the best wife in the world. But I explain to him: 'This cannot be,' I say, 'because already I have the best wife in the world.'

So he says: 'In that case, old man, Wassail to you too,' and we decide we are both very lucky guys. Just then, however, they bring in a boyo who is a minstrel, with an instrument that looks like a cross between a zither and a Welsh harp that has woodworm. The minstrel is wearing such trousers that you cannot tell whether he grows out of them, or whether the tailor just happens to be short of cloth. That is to say, they finish just above the knee, and it makes me want to sing 'Knees up Mother Brown', but they explain to me that this aria is not yet written so I cannot sing it.

The minstrel then starts up with his roundelay and I wish to state that it makes me very unhappy, but it is not his fault. For, whilst he is roundelaying, some of these characters round about are Wassailing, and the rest of them are shush-shushing.

Personally I think this denotes diabolical ignorance. Also the minstrel is singing in the manner of these times, which is to sound as if there is wind somewhere he cannot shift, so we call him 'Thunderguts'. But this is in no manner or form intended to be disrespectful, as it is most discouraging to perform under such conditions, and obviously he must pull a lot of noise from somewhere to make himself heard at all.

After he finishes and goes home, and I don't blame him, somebody who is a complete stranger comes up to me and calls me Ben the same as if he knows me for years and he says to me: 'It is your turn to sing now' he says.

I am not too sure whether he is trying to take the old Michael, or whether he is told that I do a bit of singing in my time, but I have too much of the mead and the claret and that to care very much, so I says, 'All right' I says, 'I will do that small thing, but the only roundelays I know are written in the modern idiot.'

'That is all right, Ben,' he says. 'You sing whatever you wish,' he says, 'for we know it will be good' he says.

And I know he is right at that. And nobody seems to mind that this jingle I sing is not written as yet because I write some of the verses myself. Even so, it is not such a jingle as I will normally sing at the Band of Hope, in spite of going all teetotal since this time last year. You might also remember that on the same outing last year there is a Scot who is more miserable than somewhat because of millions of acres of heather where they cannot get a living.

Well obviously this mead and claret and that is most nuclear in its potency, because this year I never see such a happy Scot and we sing 'I dream of Jeannie with the light brown hair' as a duet, but unfortunately I do not know this as good as the jingle I write myself, and maybe I am not as much help to this Scot as I ought to be.

Even so, he is now so happy I don't think he cares.

Well, it is now getting late and it is time to go home. So we all say goodnight and go out into the cold night air, and I must find out one day what is in the recipe for this mead and claret.

Most certainly it is all very confusing because although I stand perfectly still the pavement is moving about every which way. Whilst I know they have moving staircases I never before notice that they have moving pavements.

What is worse, there is a big lamp post nearby which is swaying about to a considerable extent, so I hold this up to stop it from falling down. Just then two policemen come along and look very happy, and they say to me as they pass, 'Goodnight, sir' in a most respectful manner, so it is obvious that they are grateful to me for holding up such a big lamp post.

I don't know much about what happens after this except that a gentleman drives me home in a big and most beautiful Rolls Royce. As he drives along he explains how he gets this wonderful car, and it all sounds quite honest, but quite frankly I don't care how he gets it, because it is such a wonderful ride as I never have before in all my life. In fact it is about the next best thing I ever want to happen to me unless it is the golden handshake.

After this I cannot remember anything at all until I wake up, which is unavoidable because there are about ten thousand Elizabethans singing roundelays in both earholes from inside my head, which is altogether a very terrible and distressing experience and I don't know whether I'm Ras Prince Monolulu or if it's Thursday.

Eventually I manage to struggle to the washbasin, and when I look in the mirror I can see that I don't look so good. Indeed I will not thank anybody at such a moment to tell me how much I enjoy myself the night before. So I push out my tongue, which looks considerably unhealthy, and then I speak to myself as follows.

I say: 'Good morning, Mr Life-and-Soul of the party' and then groan some more. But it does not make me feel any better, so I decide to go to the Dairy Show and I immediately meet up with a character from the night before. And believe me, brothers, this character is really sick.

So, bad as I feel myself, I try to cheer him up a bit by saying: 'Ha-ha, and Wassail to you too.' But he isn't having any. He's had it. So I preach him a very happy little sermon and I says to him like this: 'Look not on the wine when it is red,' I says, 'for at the last it biteth like a serpent and stingeth like a adder.'

But he is not impressed, and he shuffles away looking extremely miserable, and I think that maybe he is stung by the adder. I know he cannot be bitten by the serpent because it is the serpent has me. I am sure of this because I feel very terrible.

Which is all there is to say except that I realise now how very right this P.R.O. character is last year to convert me to becoming a teetotaller, and I am very grateful to him this year for proving to me that he is right.

Or, as my great Elizabethan contemporary, Billy Shakespeare used to say: 'If they have you once, shame on them. If they have you twice, shame on you.'

You can take it from me, brothers. They won't do it a third time.

Welsh Farm News, 6 January 1962

You will remember that I am now strictly teetotal at all times because of what happens when I am in London for the Dairy Show with my friend the P.R.O. Even so there are many other ways in which enjoyment may be had, and I now propose to tell you therefore and wherefore of how I enjoy myself when I am again in London for the Smithfield Show.

One evening I go to a big dinner where some bright boyo is giving it out hot and heavy on the old efficiency lark with a bit more thrown in about subsidies for good measure. It seems that in his spare time he flogs fertiliser to one and all which he is qualified to do because he once belongs to the Inland Revenue.

Obviously this makes him an expert on all matters and he goes on to explain that there is a coalmine in South Wales where the colliers are not digging enough coal to supply themselves with their own free issue. It is because of this that farming is very inefficient.

Well, naturally, this sort of stuff makes me feel pretty sick, and I can't see it will help him to sell much fertiliser, but that's his business. However, it does not drive me to drink, which is on account of my now being teetotal. Even so, I must go somewhere to be cheered up, so I decide to go to the opera.

I always think this is a good thing to do, for I am a great one for the old doh-ray-me, and at all times believeth that some music is sweet balm to a troubled soul. I also persuade a friend of mine to come with me, and he lives up on the top of a high mountain so he never sees an opera.

Well, we go to this place and the man in charge of the band comes in wearing a white shirt and taps his stick on the banister and up goes the curtain and they are able to start.

First of all the old basso comes in, and he is very quickly followed by a very big soprano indeed, but who singeth in a voice most sweet and beautiful. Shortly after this the first big moment arrives and in comes the tenor. He is a little tall fellow because he has big blocks under his heels like we use to keep the tractor up tight against the saw bench and other such operations. Even so this tenor is obviously no mug when it comes to the old doh-ray-me, and if he will write this column for me every week I will be very happy to sing his part for him if I have such a voice as he has.

In fact I think this will be a very good idea, for I have much more of the figure to match up with the soprano, and there is also another young lady round and about who looks as though she might also be another very good soprano one day, but at the moment is a real smart little piece of homework.

The whole thing now gets under way with the entrance of a gypsy who is a real nut case, because she throws a baby on the fire, which is such wickedness that I think she should be locked up in spite of having a very nice voice.

The plot then thickens and there is some very neat sword play, and the soprano goes off to join a convent, but the tenor hides in the shadows and all is well, after which the chorus people come in dressed in short vests and things made from old cake bags and sing a very good number whilst pounding on some anvils and making ye olde sparks fly every which way.

In between times the curtain comes down and the lights go up so that the audience can go out to save getting thirsty, and we also do this, for apart from the fact that when you are in Rome you do as the Romans do, even if you are teetotal there is no need to carry things to excess.

But then a bell rings and we all go back in and the opera continues. It is now obviously hotting up, for the other side, who have a very nice baritone to lead them, all come in and put the 'fluence on the gypsy, and although we are on the side of the tenor we can appreciate the other lot's point-of-view because of this gypsy burning the small harmless baby, and I will always be a party to locking up such people no matter how nice a voice they have. In any case it turns out this is only a trap to catch the tenor, which same they do very easily.

Next comes some more good doh-ray-me passages, with the tenor inside the prison and the soprano outside. Then they are all inside the prison together, and the soprano takes poison and dies, and the baritone comes in and orders the tenor to have his head chopped off which then takes place.

At the same time the gypsy really does her nut completely and the curtain comes down on a scene which looks like a commercial for somebody's louse powder. But before we have time to finish clapping and shouting 'bravo', such as is the custom in these places, the curtain goes up again and there they all are standing there with the tenor on his blocks of wood and his head back on again, and the soprano has recovered from the poison and has a big bunch of flowers, and so has the gypsy who is smiling and looking quite sensible.

Now maybe you think this all sounds very foolish, but I need only say that as we are coming out my friend says to me, 'When are we coming to London again for we must make a point of going to see some more of these little tenors and big sopranos? They are very good, and it is such beautiful music.'

And I can only say that if anybody gives me a choice between going to see the opera, or listening to well-fed fertiliser people trying to sell their wares to farmers by calling them inefficient, I know which I will choose any day.

What is more, the guy who writes the opera is a boyo called Verdi, who also spends much of his time being a farmer, so I do not think we are all such clots at that.

Welsh Farm News, 9 June 1962

It is altogether a very pleasant thought to realise that the show season is with us once again and we can have the odd day off in convivial company when there is usually quite a considerable amount of ye merry jest.

In fact I am a great believer in ye merry jest as being an institution quite harmless which doeth considerable good to one and all. It is often much in evidence at showtime because all sorts of humorous characters come up to me and say: 'I have a screaming jest for you to put in your paper.'

Usually this is at the expense of some other poor nut and is a type of one-upmanship because in due course it is quite certain that this other poor nut in turn will come up to me and say: 'Yes, that is very funny what you have in your paper and I have a good idea who tells you, and now I have a screaming jest to end all jests for you to put in your paper.'

I do not always listen to what these characters have to say because it will not be beyond some of them to make ye merry jest at my expense. They are a tough crowd. I am very pleased, however, to meet one of them this year hanging about amongst the pig lines at the first show to which I go, which sounds awkward but is good grammar.

So I says to him: 'What are you doing here, or have you been judging today?'

And he says to me: 'Oh, no. Not today. I have not been judging today. But,' he says, 'I will be judging later on this year, and so I think I will come here today to see how they should be placed, so I will know exactly how to place them when my turn comes ha ha.'

This is obviously a great joke and we both laugh hearty. But it is not very long before he has the smile wiped off his face, because the proper judge for the day has a big problem on his hands because there is a pig of his own breeding in the ring, and it is a source of great embarrassment to him to know where to place this pig of his own breeding.

Naturally he thinks this is a very fine pig indeed and will very much like to put him first because it is such a good pig. However, he thinks this might not look quite the thing to do, so he calls in my friend to say whether he should place this pig second or not.

My friend, however, takes one look at this pig and says: 'I place this pig bottom and that is my final decision.'

So my friend who is the official judge says: 'But this pig which I breed is a very good pig indeed.'

And my friend who is called in says: 'Oh, yes, most truly do I agree with you, but unfortunately for this pig which you breed, the other pigs are even better. It is my final decision.'

Naturally such a happening as this calls for a little conference in the tent afterwards where everybody is anxious to replenish his neighbour's glass and it is altogether a happy show.

Now I am not saying that all this good fellowship will be the cause of what I am about to tell you, but am content to state the facts and allow you to draw your own conclusions.

Before anybody realises what the time is there is a loudspeaker announcement saying for all the prize-winners please to have their cattle ready to come into the ring for the grand parade. Unfortunately, there is one character there who is all at sixes and sevens and in great confusion which holds up the entire proceedings whatever.

Eventually with a bit of encouragement here and there, together with a smattering of bawdy advice from his next of kin he gets things under control and the grand parade takes place. This incident comes as a great surprise to one and all, because this character is himself the Secretary to a local show in his spare time and is known to hold very strong views on such matters.

In fact, he frequently says, people should not have the cheek to enter cattle for a show unless they are prepared to honour their commitments and to use a bit of intelligence, if they have any, in getting things ready so that the thing can be run properly.

It is generally agreed, however, that the only thing to do in such cases is for a man to have his wife to help him, and it is no good at all for such a person to go away on his own without having his wife with him to tell him how to do the job properly and keep him up to scratch. And on this occasion this character's ever-loving has to stay home to do the milking, so he is naturally late for the grand parade.

I am thinking about all this on my way out of the show-ground when another of these characters comes up to me laughing like a fool and says: 'I have a screaming jest for you to put in your paper,' he says.

'There is one of these bright young things just now standing up by the sheep lines,' he says, 'and another bright young thing is talking to her,' he says, 'and one of these bright young things says to the other which sheep does she think will be the one that produces virgin wool, and the first bright young thing says it must be the one that can run the fastest.'

So this character says to me: 'Don't you think that is a screaming jest to put in your paper?'

And I say no I don't think so and I don't believe him. In fact, I shudder to think what sort of paper some of them will make of it if I listen to half of what they tell me.

Welsh Farm News, 30 June 1962

I wish to write for you this week about the sort of thing which can happen on almost any farm and sometimes does, and moreover it goes to prove how careful tractor drivers and such characters should be at all times. I don't know exactly how it happens. That is to say, I don't know whether the tractor slips out of gear, or if the brakes pack up, or whether the character who is on board misjudges the distance or what. But it seems that all of a sudden the machine is rattling down-hill at a speed sharper than somewhat. Furthermore the tractor goes slap dab into the hedge, and there is the subject who has been driving it flat out on the grass verge and looking as if he doesn't know whether they are haymaking or if it's Sunday.

At this precise moment of time, however, a ministering angel appears upon the scene in the shape of a passing postman, who hurls himself upon the dislodged tractor driver with great force and holds him down before he has a chance to rise and aggravate his grievous hurt.

'You must not move,' says the postman. 'Indeed if you move it might well prove to be fatal for you. Furthermore,' he states, 'it is indeed fortunate for you that I arrive at this moment, because I have great experience at this sort of emergency and have attended night classes and learnt all about it to a considerable extent.'

'In fact,' he says, 'when I am in London I have much practice at this business in the air raids, and I wear a tin hat and also have a band on my arm, likewise also I have a whistle and a gas mask. It is because of this that I am now insisting that you make no attempt to move.'

The postman then makes his diagnosis and states that this subject has a very badly fractured pelvis, and the subject groans when he hears this because only the year before he has a cow which sustains this self-same injury and they have to have her shot.

The postman also goes on to state that there are various other matters which are causing him some concern, so that the subject lying on the grass verge groans worse than ever as he realises from the long words and medical terms which the postman uses that he must be in a very bad way, and then some.

Anyway, the postman calls to the first passer-by and sends her off to telephone in great urgency, which same she does forthwith with commendable alacrity and calls for an ambulance. She also explains about the fractured pelvis, so they say to her now wait a minute and how does she know all this.

So she explains to them how lucky they are the postman has such qualifications, and they say all right they will send the ambulance. The ambulance arrives and takes the subject into hospital with a great clanging of bells, and they put him on a trolley, and there is a great smell of carbolic everywhere, not to mention white linen and sharp knives and all this and that, which are always to be found in such places.

In no time at all there is a doctor on the job, and he proceeds to give the patient a very good going over indeed. And when he finishes he says: 'This is a remarkably healthy man and very fit. It is obvious to me that he leads an active outdoor life and therefore I assume he is a farmer. They are always very healthy people. But what is more,' he says, 'this subject is sound in wind and limb, and there is no break or fracture in any manner, shape or form. Will you please say why he has been brought in here?'

So then some more characters look at him and say obviously he is suffering from a great shock, and they treat him for this to make him better. Then they let him go home.

It now becomes obvious to one and all that this subject is only winded in the first place, and the shock is brought on when the postman nearly frightens him to death by jumping on him and using long words which remind him of what happens to his cow and how they have to shoot her.

I hear about this one day when I am at a meeting, and a character gets up under any other business, which is an item where all sorts of bods can either make ye merry jest or speak great foolishness, and sometimes you cannot tell the difference, and when he finishes one and another say what is he talking about, and who the hell is he?

And somebody else says: 'Do you never hear what happens when they take some poor fellow to hospital because they understand he fractures his pelvis?'

It is then the story comes out, and that is why I know about this.

Which is all there is to say, except to state that the moral is very clear.

And the moral is that it is a good thing to know about first aid, but as far as possible, it is better not to fall off the tractor in the first place.

Welsh Farm News, 18 August 1962

I hope you will not read this column this week as it is nothing but a great deal of foolishness about something very nebulous, which as I explain to you before means without foundation.

I am thus prompted by a report in a national paper this week which screams to the world – 'Grey-rumped sandpiper is a "phoney".'

The report then goes on to state that some character who once lives in Sussex was supposed to have come across a lot of rare birds in that area, but it now looks as if he had them brought into the country on ice from the foreign parts where they used to flit about a bit and whistle a merry tune.

As this character has now been dead for about twenty years, however, I do not suppose he minds very much what they say about him, and I'll bet he has a good old laugh in his time. You will understand from what I previously tell you that these birdy types are very serious indeed with their rings and measurements and what not. Certainly they will be much disturbed to learn that the grey-rumped sandpiper and many other such rarities are nothing but the old phonus bolonus.

Furthermore, I know something about the old phonus bolonus myself and likewise write little pieces for you on the odd occasion about all such strange birds as the mugwump, the elephant bird, the mustard bird and, now and again, the oozlum bird.

I am very interested in this most recent case of the old phonus bolonus, however, as I think it might explain something which troubles some of us in these parts for a good many years.

Once upon a time there is a character writing a few pieces about this and that round the islands of West Wales to try to earn a crust, and he also writes down in his book each day about the birds which are all round and about the place. He also gives instructions to the trapper who is catching rabbits for him on the island, and also the two lads who are helping the trapper, to take note of all creatures unusual so that he can record all facts about them in his book.

Well, on this occasion, Master has gone away in the boat to the take his rabbits to the mainland and he is gone for a day and a night and returns late in the afternoon on the following day. So after supper Master gets out his book to write down what you might call the vital statistics and he says, 'Now,' he says, 'what is there to report and what do you see whilst I am away?'

So the trapper takes his pipe out of his mouth and spits in the fire till the bars sizzle more than somewhat and he says, 'Well there's nothing very much to report except about the little bord.' You must also understand that such characters as the one to whom I am referring, pronounce it 'bord' in this part of the world although me and thee who have had the benefit of this here edecation would call it 'bird'.

So Master pricks up his ears and says very excited, 'What bird was this? What bird?'

So the trapper says, 'Oh, 'twas a pretty little bord. Had a bit of red on her head an' blue down her belly an' all green under her wings with all yellow spots an' a lot of white an' her tail was . . . '

'Yes,' says Master sharpish, 'where was it?'

'Well I'll tell thee now,' says the trapper, 'I'd pulled up the traps down south side an' I thinks to myself 'tis hardly worth settin' these again now with Master bein' off in case the weather comes up rough an' he don't come back with the boat so off I goes to have a look at the traps up over beyond th'owld well. An' that's when I seen the little bord.'

'Where was she?' says Master.

'Why,' says the trapper, 'there she was in the trap. An' oh she was a pretty little bord. She had a bit of red on her head an' blue down her . . . '

'Yes, all right,' says Master getting a bit curly because of the slow way the story is being told, 'where is the bird now?'

'Well that's what I'm trying to tell you,' says the trapper. 'I could see as she was dead, so . . . '

'Well if she was dead,' shouts master, getting very worked up indeed, 'where is she now? Let me see her at once.'

So the trapper takes his pipe out of his mouth and has another spit which goes right between the fire bars this time and then he says, 'Now that's what I'm tryin' to tell you but I don't see how I can tell you if you're gwain to keep on interruptin'.'

So Master bites his lip and tries very hard to stay quiet and be patient. So the trapper starts off again, 'So like I towld you I'd pulled up the traps down south side an' I thinks to myself 'tis hardly worth settin' 'em. Well I towld you what I thought like, so I went over to the traps beyond th'owld well an' there was the little bord in the trap.'

So the trapper looks at Master, but Master is obviously listening patiently and is showing no sign of interrupting again, so the trapper goes on to describe the bird again and in fact adds a few more colours and spots which he doesn't think of the first time.

'So now then,' says the trapper, 'I thinks to myself Master'll surely want to see this'll' bord because I knows how you likes writin' down all about the little bords in the book every night. So I takes her out of the trap an' puts her in my pockat. For you to see her.'

'Well now then,' says Master between his teeth, 'let me see her.'

'That's just it,' says the trapper. 'I haven't got her.'

'Haven't got her,' screams Master. 'Then where is she?'

'Well it's like I said,' says the trapper. 'I knowed as you'd want to see her so I put her up there on the mantelpiece. An', oh, she was a pretty little bord. A bit of red on her head an' blue . . . '

'Where is she now?' wails Master with fire in his eyes and his mouth open and dribble running down his chin. 'Where is she now?'

'Well that's like I said,' says the trapper. 'I put her there on the mantelpiece for I knowed you'd want to see her an' there she was last night when we went to bed. But she was gone this mornin'.'

'Gone!' raves Master. 'How could she be gone if she was dead!'

'Ah,' says the trapper, 'the mice must have had her.'

Foolish this column may be. Yes, and many other of the adjectives you might see fit to apply to it. But we have never yet given it over to obscenity. So I can't really tell you of the oaths which shatter the island peace that night.

Maybe it doesn't matter very much, but it's odd how the thought comes back after all these years.

In fact it is beginning to look as if the trapper is no better than some of these birdy types, and I'm thinking his bird must go into the record books with the grey-rumped sandpiper and all that lot.

I don't know whether it is ever entered in Master's book or not, but if you ask me this bird is nothing but the old phonus bolonus.

Welsh Farm News, 27 October 1962

I'm still no wiser than ever over this business of the Common Market, but as far as I can make out from what everybody tells me, we're going in. That does not mean that there will not be ceaseless argument, and if politicians can't agree in one language, I don't see how they can hope to agree in a large number of different languages.

Furthermore I think they will have a very big job on their hands at that, because I remember what a hell of a time we had in the Parish Council when we tried to get together for the Coronation celebrations. Truly it was a most joyous occasion and a good time was had by all. But not without a few harsh words being spoken.

The Parish Council took the initiative through the medium of a parish meeting, and that was a mistake in the first place. We didn't get out until after shut-tap, and copper boy had warned us he'd be round with the sergeant, so there was no chance of a quick one, and all we'd done was to end up by deciding to have a committee of two representatives from each organisation in the parish.

With one church and five chapels, that accounted for a dozen or so to start with. By the time one and another had said Women's Institute, Mothers' Union, Y.F.C., Football Club, Darts Club, Improvement Committee, Hall Committees and goodness only knows what else, we had a much bigger *ad hoc* committee than if we'd elected the entire parish meeting *en bloc.*

Now I am a great believer in the W.I. They are a very fine organisation which doeth much good work. Unfortunately, most of their best members were on the committee representing some of the other organisations. And about the only one who wasn't on from some other organisation was a regular old harridan and hell-cat. So they sent her.

I do not wish to state that we all agree on every subject in the Parish Council, and in fact I have heard some harsh words spoken there on more than one occasion. But there is a strict rule that we must be out before shut-tap for obvious reasons.

And when things get a bit hot and strong under 'any other business' it is remarkable how it can be straightened out afterwards under the mellowing influence of a glass or two. So what with one thing and another, and a bit of understanding, we get along pretty fairish in the Parish Council, and also put up a few stiles and trim the odd footpath now and again in order to improve the standard of living for one and all.

But when we were pitched into the hurly-burly of the Coronation Celebration Committee we were just about ready to abdicate. That was a christening, brothers. I'll tell you now. That was a christening.

The Chairman met his Waterloo the first night in the saddle when he was explaining what the District Council was prepared to do which included the provision of the mugs suitable to such occasions.

We'd never thought that the R.D.C. were much good at all and the offer looked like giving us a good start. But as soon as the Chairman had said his piece, one ancient character who'd retired to the parish after years of promoting the interests of the Empire in foreign climes, ups and says: 'I move we accept the offer of mugs from the R.A.C.'

Then he went on to say that he was a member of the A.A. himself and he certainly intended to take the matter up with them to see why they weren't making a similar offer. Unfortunately, this old fool was an ardent member of the Conservative Party and had recently been plodding round the parish with their latest pamphlets, so they'd put him on our C.C.C. as one of their representatives.

On a point of principle the senior nominee of the Labour Party felt it was her duty to argue with him. After that we got on to religion and, church and chapel both having refused to give way, we got bogged down on where, if at all, we could hold a united open air service to the glory of the Almighty with a special prayer for Her Gracious Majesty.

At this stage we broke up into two committees. We had to. Time was getting short. And that's where old Sally Harridan came into it. On the catering. She wanted us to have boiled ham. And she knew where we could get a good one because her daughter had one to sell at seven-and-sixpence per pound.

We argued the point at first, but she didn't care a damn about facts and figures and weight and how many to be served or how much each we'd get per head. She wouldn't even be thwarted when the Chairman, on behalf of the Parish Council, who were more concerned about the liquid refreshments, tried to confuse the issue by talking about 'the product of a fourpenny rate'. It was, she said, 'something to cut at'. Mercifully it went by default in the end because nobody would volunteer to boil it.

In the event things went rather well. Old Sally Harridan grumbled in the corner with her family round her (she never had any friends in her life) which was the only way she knew in which to enjoy herself.

In the excitement of the arrival of another bundle of Tory pamphlets from the local agent, who had just been appointed and was making early preparations to lose the next election, the ancient Empire builder forgot about his threat to cancel his membership of the A.A. and join the R.A.C. instead.

Furthermore, in direct contrast to old Sally

Harridan's boiled ham, the Parish Council were re-elected by default *en bloc*, because when our term of office expired nobody came out against us, and the Chairman said there were statutory regulations to cover such contingencies.

Which is about all there is to say, and I hope and trust that the politicians will not have a bigger problem to deal with in the Common Market than old Sally Harridan and her boiled ham.

Furthermore I wish to state that if a loyal subject can try to wreck the organisation of such a worthy cause as joyful celebrations concerning Her Gracious Majesty on account of wanting to flog her daughter's ham, then I will not trust some of these foreign characters when there is no knowing what they wish to flog.

Welsh Farm News, 10 November 1962

You will be pleased to learn that I am safe returned from the big, bad City following visit annual to the Dairy Show. Furthermore I now propose to write a little piece for you about same and hope and trust you will not find it amusing. In fact it is a great calamity.

Indeed it is even more of a calamity because I get into such bad company at last year's Dairy Show that I am now almost teetotal. And I get to thinking that, no matter how much I ever hit the old grape juice with my very good friend the P.R.O., nothing so diabolical ever happens to me before, and I cannot see there is much percentage in being teetotal at that.

However, I had better start at the beginning and explain that I do not wish to get into bad company, and therefore I buy myself two tickets to go to the opera so that I will have a good excuse for not becoming mixed up with some doubtful characters such as P.R.O.'s and that and, what is more, I am a great lover of the old doh-ray-me.

Although many of the characters who are normally very pleased to come to the opera with me any time I have a spare ticket are all fixed up with some other arrangements, I find a companion eventually who is also a great lover of the old doh-ray-me and we set off for the opera.

Well, we get to the place and it really is something, with velvet curtains and gold paint and what-have-you, and most of the customers are dressed up to somewhere.

Then the head-boss man of the band comes in, the lights go down, the curtain goes up and the opera begins to commence. The story is about a lot of layabouts who live in an attic and never seem to do an honest day's work, but just do a bit of painting in a temper, and maybe write some poetry and all that sort of jazz.

Then, when they have written the poetry they put it in the stove and burn it to be able to keep warm, so maybe it is not very good poetry at that. In point of fact the poet is none other than the tenor in the opera, and this is the first surprise, because he is quite a smart and upstanding sort of tenor. And normally, as I tell you before, the tenor is usually a little tall fellow by virtue of the blocks under his heels like we use under the tractor wheels to keep the belt up tight against the sawbench.

However, I am bound to state that I hear better tenors in my time, especially among the little tall fellows, but even so it is sweet music most beautiful to listen to, and there is a useful basso, and the fiddles in the band are scraping away in a very tender manner. Indeed it is my favourite opera, and although I see it many times I still hope to see it a good many more.

The rest of the opera is taken up with the soprano, who is dying from consumption when she is not looking for her key in the dark because her candle goes out. This is because they have no electric light at the time the opera is written, neither is there an attested herd scheme started at this time, which is why the poor soprano has consumption.

Now it is customary in opera for sopranos to die of consumption and usually they are very big sopranos indeed. But although I see bigger sopranos than this one in my time I do not think she is such a soprano as I will want to fall on top of me if she rolls off a load of hay some time. There is plenty of her, although a good bit of it is pulled in here and there.

This is not such a tragic opera as some others which I see from time to time, however. There is no sword play or poisoning, and nobody dies off in the first act, or even the second. In fact nobody dies until the very end when the soprano expires on account of the consumption, and it takes the entire opera for her to get round to it.

What is more, in between fits of coughing and right up to the time she finally dies, she manages to belt it out on the old doh-ray-me. In fact, she is as good a soprano as I ever hear, or very nearly.

So that explains about the opera and the attested herd scheme. I also wish to state that when we go to quench our thirst in the intervals we do it with orange squash, and I hope you will believe me because of what happens later.

Well, we come out of the opera and go into the street and then turn left again. Before we know it there are lorries everywhere, because this is the famous market and you never see so many Brussels-sprouts, cabbages, celery, potatoes and all the rest of it in all your Nelly.

Whereupon my companion says it is a funny place to have an opera house, but I say it is a funnier so-and-so place to have a market, and I quote the ancient riddle of which came first, the apple or the pip. Naturally I then put my hands in my pockets as we walk along and I begin to hold forth.

And any time I get the bit between my teeth in this manner there is no need for anyone to interrupt, answer back or keep the argument going in any shape or form. I can manage. Especially when I am on a favourite subject such as this which concerns efficiency. In fact I say that it is monstrous that people should be allowed to talk to farmers about efficiency, when all the time this sinful waste is being tolerated, creating bottle-necks, wasting time, damaging the produce and so on and so forth, and what is more I propose to write a very powerful piece about this immediately upon my return.

It is most unfortunate, however, that just at this moment we are crossing from one dimly lit corner to another, when all of a sudden I get my heel on an old banana skin and go bass over aria *poco poco agitato*. I land with a most desperate thud slap dab on my elbow and one other place.

Whilst the road is hard and the pavement likewise, being made of stone, it so happens that I have the added misfortune to fall on the kerb, which is made of granite. And if you know of anything harder than granite to fall on I will avoid it at all costs. It is certainly very terrible.

There are two characters, male and female, just behind, dressed in the manner of very high class opera goers, and they are greatly concerned on my account when they see me fall because they have enough sense to know that it is such a fall as will normally kill a person, or at any rate put him unconscious for a very great length of time, unless he is drunk, because it is a fact which is well-known to one and all that drunks have the most remarkable escapes.

So when they see me struggling to rise, because I am not such a badger as likes to attract too much attention, they immediately decide I must be drunk and walk round me just as if I am a crate of rotten cabbages. This is why I say there is no percentage in being teetotal, because you have my word for it I only drink orange juice all the evening.

I must also state, albeit with considerable sorrow, that as I rise to my feet and it becomes evident that it is not quite an ambulance case, my companion goes off into fits of hysterical laughter, because the world is full of ignorance and lack of feeling.

There is no more to state on this subject except that when I arrive home I look to see what is in *Welsh Farm News* and find that the writer of Talking Points is on about litter louts, and I reckon I can add a bit to what he has to say at that.

In the same issue Magpie is chattering about footwork and I deeply regret that he jumps the gun in this manner, because if only he knows about my little piece of choreography at the back of the opera house he will really have something worth writing about.

In fact you are all very lucky that I survive to write for you as I do, and I hope and trust that you will never decide to become teetotal if anything half as bad is likely to happen to you.

Welsh Farm News, 22 June 1963

I wish to write for you this week about sex.

This may come as a great surprise to you, but as far as I can make out it is one certain way to get everybody to read the column, because by all accounts it is a pastime which occupies a great deal of the leisure hours of all sorts of characters here and there, and it is a subject about which everybody is always wanting to read. Then, after they've read it, they can always say what a terrible press we have. But, if you ask me, it's just as well we have press types round and about to uncover some of these shenanigans at that.

I also wish to make it clear that I do not propose to write about the problem of whether fertiliser should be packed in hundredweight sacks or half-hundredweight sacks. What I wish to write about is sex with three letters, and the real Adam and Eve stuff at that, and no mucking about with the old apple tree.

And it so happens that it is necessary for me to write for you on this subject because of the politicians, and it is well-known to one and all that I often write about the politicians although I am never very complimentary about same. In fact I hear tell of a worried mother the other day who tells her husband that he isn't shouldering his parental responsibilities as he should and it is high time he tells his growing lad all about the birds and the bees.

So the old man puts the paper down and takes his pipe out of his mouth and tells Johnny to stop playing with the tom cat because he wishes to explain about the birds and the bees. And Johnny says what about the birds and the bees, and the old man says: 'You know all this stuff that's been on the telly and in the papers lately about the politicians. Well, the birds and the bees do the same.'

In fact, when one farmer's wife reads all about the scandal, she has the biggest shock she ever has since her husband says he has to go away on a course, and she finds out after that the only course he is ever on is a racecourse, and the only course he ever takes is his sexual inter. Which just goes to show you that nobody's any better than anybody else, which is evident after what is in the paper about some parson or other not long ago, and far be it from me to sit in judgement on the morals of politicians or anybody else and go about the place saying they did not ought to have done it, because they always reckon you can do what you like with your own.

But when a politician, and a Tory at that, says Tory honour has been besmirched and that he is sick of seeing the newspapers and TV screens full of the sordid details of the farmyard morals and pigsty habits of certain members of the community, of whom he believes there are too many in high places, it is time for some straight talking.

I hope I will never be a party to cruelty to dumb animals, and likewise, when dumb animals are being slandered and cannot answer back, I feel minded to put in a word on their behalf. Furthermore, I would state that, if we could be sure that our politicians were behaving as well as our farmyard animals, we would not have much cause to worry about the sort of image they are creating or what sort of security risk they are.

The offending M.P. is Sir Cyril Osborne, who is reported as having made these derogatory references to the farmyard animals when speaking in his constituency of Louth in Lincolnshire. I don't know anything about his qualifications as a politician and, for all I know, he's probably a good husband and a kind father. But he certainly doesn't know much about the ways and habits of the farmyard.

Pigsty habits, he said. Every pig I ever knew usually kept a nice clean bed in one corner and used another corner, outside if possible, as a lavatory. But the way some of these here high-up what-nots have been polluting their own nests of late is enough to make you think.

In fact if you say of people they haven't the brains of a goose it is understood by one and all that you are speaking with great disrespect. But the geese at least keep to their own partners and so do many other feathered birds, sometimes for life, and what I always say is that it's a pity to judge the feathered birds by some of the other birds we read about.

Most of our cows only ever want to go to bull once a year and don't bother much about that sort of thing in between times, so nobody can call that over-indulgence. Furthermore, when our old bull goes into action there is always an end product in view, and he certainly doesn't come straight back and then try to deny that he's been there, because if he did you'd never know which cow was in-calf to what, and the pedigree records would get in one hell of a mess.

And, what's more, the farmyard animals don't have a call-girl racket, but they do have a call-boy racket, which is known as the bull with the bowler hat. It isn't their fault though, and I've heard it said that they're not all that happy about it, and it's quite a racket at that, because the members of National Milk Records have to provide all the information to prove what wonderful bulls are standing at A.I. centres and pay top price for the privilege of doing so.

Indeed the more I think about these matters the more puzzled I become. But one evening this week I went to see our sheep along with another character, and the stupid things were just getting through the hedge into the barley. And I says to this character:

'What on earth can you say is the matter with such stupid creatures that they are not content in all this beautiful fresh grass, but they must go and break through into the barley?'

And this character says to me: 'Of course,' he says, 'some of these politicians have very pretty wives,' he says. So I says: 'Maybe you're right,' I says, 'so maybe I must be glad they only break into the barley.'

After all is said and done it could have been worse. They might have broken into the hayfield.

And when I came into breakfast this morning I started to say something about politicians, and Mrs Brock said: 'Not in front of the child, dear.'

Furthermore I am writing in this vein because I read somewhere the other day it is more rewarding to be a comic than to be serious. I don't know about rewarding, but I know there are always two ways of looking at anything.

And if you don't laugh you can only do the other thing. And when I cry about something I want it to be something worthwhile. And you can take it from me, friends, that it isn't this lot no matter what they have done to bring the morals of the farmyard into disrepute.

It would, however, be most unfortunate if, while discussing sex and farmyard morals, we allowed this squalid scandal to cause anyone to lose sight of our real grievance which is the present Government's treatment of agriculture.

Welsh Farm News, 7 December 1963

More's the pity, and to my great sorrow, there has come my way a handbook called, 'Introduction to Management' and which would appear to have been foisted upon an unsuspecting public by the Min. of Ag. and Fish. (and Food).

It is part of a more comprehensive omnibus called 'The Farm as a Business'. The frightening thought is that there are another seven such efforts still to come. The 'puff' that goes with it says that it is a step forward in providing farmers and farm advisers with the data needed for efficient management.

Now I don't know anything about the farm advisers. But you can take it from me, friends, I've got enough troubles of my own. Too many troubles, that is to say, than to have time to wade through this lot. As they say where I come from, it would need a Philadelphia lawyer to uncaffle it.

Mind you, it's probably, for all I know, quite a good book. Who am I to judge? Especially when no less a person than the Minister of Ag. and Fish. (and Food) his very own self in person says in a Foreword that this book is just about the cat's whiskers. So there you are, I haven't read it. And I'll tell you for why. I just don't have brains to that extent.

The Introduction is all right insofar as it does no more than pass the time of day. In the first paragraph of the book proper, the second sentence says that: 'It is generally assumed that farm businesses are planned for the maximum profit consistent with good husbandry.' This is a most noble sentiment, and I am all for it. But definitely. All for it.

The second sentence, however, has a sideways little swipe at the show-ring, and my bristles rise ever so slightly. The third sentence comes out with that jangling term so beloved of them what would presume to teach their grandmas to suck eggs, 'profit maximisation'.

At the sight of it I feared the worst, and it wasn't long in coming.

Let me admit that no-one is more conscious of my shortcomings as a farmer than I am. And you can all testify to the fact that I am a very ignorant journalist what cannot hardly write nor read the Queen's English not nohow. But, I asks you. Just listen to this.

There is a bit about the price of milk and the cost of concentrates, and then there is some more about the cost of hiring a beet harvester compared with casual hand labour. Reading this through three or four times, and more slowly each time, I think that maybe I can see what they are driving at, although it doesn't put me in the frame of mind to be recommending it as a best-seller.

Having waded through this lot, however, I read as follows:

'These examples are relatively straightforward.' So help me. And if you read the next paragraph you can maybe understand why. For this is what it says: 'In other cases the choice of a least-cost combination of inputs is more complicated, particularly when a combination of inputs, rather than two direct substitutes, is involved.

'For example, a dairy cow may be fed various combinations of hay and concentrates, or a pig can be fattened on various proportions of grain and protein supplement.

'When there is a diminishing rate of substitution between various inputs the least-cost combination, which involves both physical relationships and relative prices, rarely leads to the exclusive use of one or other of the ingredients. In these circumstances, the cheapest combination of resources will be found when the value of any resource replaced is just greater than the value of the resource introduced.'

I am willing to admit that, at this stage, my enthusiasm began to wane more than somewhat, with the result that the next page or so didn't perhaps register quite as much as it should have done. Then, at last, I came to this piece of imperishable prose. The scales fell before my eyes, and with awful, soul-searching clarity, night became day, and the way was pointed clear before me.

I'll quote it for you. As writ:

'The most sophisticated of these techniques is linear programming. It provides a means of estimating the optimum production programme for a farm by relating the gross margin per unit of production (which comprises the gross output less variable costs) for a series of activities or enterprises to a given set of fixed resources or restrictions. The relationships between specific farming activities and the restrictions on them are expressed in algebraic terms and are solved according to a procedure known as the Simplex method which proceeds from an initial feasible plan to a final optimum solution.

'In a farm planning problem with a considerable number of production possibilities and a range of restrictions, the actual computations may be an onerous matter. Fortunately the introduction of the linear programming technique to farming has coincided with the development of electronic computers, so that computations which would otherwise take days to solve can now be made in a matter of minutes. Although linear programming uses constant input-output coefficients (gross margin per acre, etc.) and all activities are additive, it is possible to make allowance in any model for varying marginal rates of substitution and diminishing returns.'

Well, I can tell you all about that bit about the diminishing returns. I can tell you all about that. And no wonder, if we have to go on slaving our guts out to keep more and more characters churning out this sort of stuff, which is supposed to be for farmers to read.

Mind you, it could be a very good book, and I won't argue that it isn't. But I hope you will understand why I just couldn't press on any further. I still haven't finished the Denning Report yet. Life is just too short for everything. No wonder my friends in the NAAS sometimes complain to me that they do not always have time to read the latest gems offered in this column because there is so much stuff (that's what they call it) which they HAVE to read. I'm sorry for them. Truly sorry. And they have all my sympathy.

But I still have the booklet, and having no intention of even trying to wade through it at some future date which would never arrive, I have to decide what to do with it. Before anybody feels like making unseemly suggestions I'll tell you what I had in mind. I thought that maybe we could take out the two little staples which fasten the middle, and then make a hole in the top left-hand corner to take a bit of string for hanging it up on a nail behind the door of some convenient little place.

In fact, I put the proposition to Mrs Brock, but she said it wouldn't be very hygienic. Rather to my surprise she never said anything about my being a vulgar badger. So maybe it's not such a bad idea at that, and we'll have use for the next seven when they arrive after all.

Welsh Farm News, 18 January 1964

*An unusual request to members of Anglesey NFU branch . . .
to help Somerset woman Mrs Pamela Sykes in her
researches. Apparently Mrs Sykes is compiling information
about working elephants in Britain and has already been told
of one farmer on the island who used one some years ago*
(Welsh Farm News, *11 January 1964).*

I see that Giraldus has made reference to a lady
wanting to find out about an elephant in Anglesey.

Well, I know all about elephants, as I know about
most things, but whether this is the same elephant I
cannot say.

This happens when the travelling circus comes to
town and a great storm blows up and demolishes the
marquee, which is pronounced mark-you by some
people, but only in fun, and the elephant breaks loose.

Well, late that night, after the storm blows itself out,
and the moon is riding high in a clear sky in a most
poetic manner indeed, a poor old lady gets out of bed
and looks through her bedroom window. And lo and
behold, which is simply another way of saying, 'Cor
blimey O'Reilly', there is this powerful great elephant
standing in her kitchen garden, and as far as she can
make out, pulling up all her cabbages with his tail, if
you ever hear of such a thing. Well, naturally, the poor
old lady is disturbed more than somewhat about this
and hurries downstairs to telephone the police.

And who should answer the 'phone but the local
sergeant himself, and so the poor old soul pours out
her troubles about the elephant being in her garden,
and will he please contact the circus people and see
about removing the elephant forthwith and most
immediate. In fact, it is very urgent.

But the sergeant, after the manner of his kind, first of

all has to write down the lady's name and her address. All of which takes a little time. This task completed, however, he says next what is the elephant doing in the garden and the lady says, 'He is pulling up all my cabbages with his tail.'

So the sergeant then writes all this down whilst the poor old lady is fuming with impatience on the other end of the line, but eventually the sergeant says, 'Well now, ma'am, tell me. What is he doing with the cabbages after he pulls them up with his tail?'

And, quite unable to stand it any longer, the poor old girl exclaims, 'If I told you, you wouldn't believe me, so come round and see for yourself.'

Whether it's the same elephant up in Anglesey I wouldn't know. But I thought I'd mention it. Just to be helpful like.

Welsh Farm News, 7 **March 1964**

I wish to write for you this week on the subject of marketing, which is a question very much in the minds of one and all at this particular moment of time as people say these days when they wish it to be known that they sometimes go to London.

Now the last time I write for you in this column I state quite frankly that I am on the old stir. But I do not wish to stir for you this week, or not much, and in any case not so that anybody will notice, but I wish to write about marketing. In fact what I wish to state is only a very small little bit of a stir indeed, and no stir can possibly be any smaller than that.

Maybe I mention to you sometime that the matter of which I wish to speak is like the old lady used to say, it is like a chip of wood in broth. There is not a lot of good in it, and not a lot of harm, but it's something to stir. And whilst all this amounts to such a very small stir, it is nevertheless a matter of which I must speak on account of marketing being such an uncommon important matter whatever.

And, if you ask me, farmers do not begin to have a clue about marketing, which is just another way of saying salesmanship. And I think we shall have to smarten up our ideas more than somewhat if we are ever going to make any big impression, because I come to the conclusion that when it comes to salesmanship there are some very smart operators about indeed.

In fact I read about some new sales stunt some little time ago about a lot of books, and I mention same to Mrs Brock and she says good gracious what do you think of that and I reply not much. The idea is that some character calls on you, or telephones you, and says he is willing to sell you books which cost about two hundred and eighty pounds.

But, states this character, you have been chosen for this special offer, and in fact you can have all these books for the giveaway ridiculously low price of one hundred pounds, if only you will tell your friends about them and maybe allow them to call on you to see what a wonderful bargain these books are.

Well, I may as well tell you that once upon a time I am foolish enough to be lumbered with a heap of books which cost forty pounds, because one small badger comes home from school and says a man calls round and says they are very good, and Miss says you will speak to your father on this matter, and this is certainly a great racket which I think will have to be stopped one day.

Well, these books have a great deal of knowledge, which is no more than you will expect for forty pounds, and amongst other things there is reference to this great character by the name of William Shakespeare, and I understand it is this gentleman who once states, 'If they have you once, shame on them. If they have you twice, shame on thee.'

So, sure enough, when some character telephones one day a little time later when I am away hithering and thithering, Mrs Brock, on account of being forewarned being forearmed, is able to state that we do not yet learn all the knowledge we buy for forty pounds, so it will surely be some time before we can think about starting on this next lot of knowledge, even at the giveaway price of one hundred pounds.

Now I am sorry I have to speak on this matter at such length, but I hope you will understand why this is necessary when I go on to speak of a more recent matter which I trust will be of interest to one and all. In fact it is a very neat line indeed, because I receive through the post a kind of certificate with fancy gilt lettering, which makes it look as though I am very honoured indeed, and which seems to hold out promise of great good fortune.

In fact it holds out promise of such great friendship and brotherhood and freedom from hunger and want for evermore that I think this is nearly all too good to be true. Because although I am a very foolish badger over many matters, I find out after many years that there are not many characters round and about who are anxious to give you something for nothing.

In fact in a book on philosophy I am once reading it is stated, and I am now old enough to pass the advice on to you, sooner or later someone is going to come up to you with a brand new pack of cards with the seal unbroken, and they will be willing to bet you that, if you will draw out the Jack of Hearts you will get an earful of apple juice. Therefore it will be just as well for you not to bet on such a proposition otherwise you are certain to end up with an earful of apple juice.

Therefore on account of all this great experience and reading such books on philosophy, which are not such books as come in the forty pounds class, I decide to telephone a friend of mine who knows more than somewhat about insurance, and I speak to him of this matter. And immediately he says it is a great racket, like the book racket, only their gimmick is to play you a gramophone record first. So as soon as he speaks of the books I am convinced and decide to await events, because all the gilt lettering says I will be approached in due course.

Sure enough, it comes on a Saturday and the telephone rings, and this character states his business and mentions the gramophone record, so I say I cannot commit myself in this matter, but I will listen to his gramophone record. So that afternoon he comes along, and I observe that he has a much nicer car than I can afford, and also a very smart suit, so I conclude there is certainly something to be said for all this fraternalism, and I can understand his being greatly in favour of same.

Well, we settle down and he puts on his gramophone record on a machine which I have for the purpose. In fact it is a machine which affords me many hours of soothing and beautiful company, and even inspiration when I am sometimes at a loss to know of what matters I might write for you. But I wish to state that my machine never plays such a gramophone record as this before. It is strictly the old phonus bolonus and then some.

Far from feeling honoured that I have been selected for admission to the circle, I come to the conclusion that they must think I am a bit of a goop and a glutton for punishment. The gramophone record starts off with some very touching music, and this is greatly in order as far as I am concerned, because it is well known to one and all that I am a firm believer in the old doh-ray-me.

But then some character starts off about travelling the road alone, and all this and that, and I commence wondering whether I am going to end up becoming a Mormon or something. But then we are down in the middle of a big wood, and some ancient character in olden times is being led blindfolded into the centre of a gathering of other fraternal characters.

However, we then leave the forest glade and hear about the great benefits which are waiting to be showered upon us, but it is necessary to believe in God and also to be physically fit. However, when the gramophone record finishes playing, the character in the smart suit states that he is now ready to answer questions, but he doesn't ask me anything at all about God.

Maybe this is because he sees the little text which

always hangs on the wall near where I write, and maybe it is because he is anxious to speak about the great benefits which are to be conferred upon me in terms of pounds, shillings and pence. But he certainly makes pointed reference more than once to the need for physical fitness, which makes me think that there is not much benefit coming the way of anybody who is very sick and likely to need it.

There is also talk of the social activities, but I explain that I get more than my share of these, and have no objection to cutting down on same instead of increasing them. So then I ask him how much all these benefits will cost me, because I realise he cannot possibly have such a nice car and a new suit and get me all these benefits unless I make some small contribution towards it all.

And what he says is that he cannot put a price on it, but will I make him an offer. Now I come across all sorts of insurance characters from time to time who have their eye on the main chance, but I never before come across one with a gramophone record, although most of them can tell a good story. In fact one of my insurance pals can tell three or four good stories in a row. He is a great character.

Furthermore this character then speaks in terms of surrender value, and I consider this to be strictly an insurance term, so that I can't see where God or the gramophone record come into it. And I see by my watch that it is just about time for wrestling on the old goggle-box, so I bid this character good-afternoon, for I do not wish to miss this fun which is greater than I am having with this boyo from the forest glade, although I keep a straight face throughout. Then he goes away in such a state that he forgets to take his gramophone record with him, and I regret to say that I do not think to record it on a tape for the amusement of my insurance pals, and he comes back a couple of hours later in a state of great agitation to retrieve it.

In any case I now have a subject on which I can write for your edification, and you will understand what I mean when I say that farmers simply haven't begun to understand what is meant by salesmanship.

Welsh Farm News, 8 August 1964

Life is full of problems and, I believe it has been remarked, is neither all sorrow nor all happiness. We have our ups and downs, everything has its compensations, and everything has its drawbacks.

It would be supposed that nothing could be more pleasant than for a man to be able to count two charming young ladies amongst his friends. But that's where it comes in about the drawbacks. Especially if he is one of the ignorant types and doesn't know about hedgehogs.

Let me explain. These two charming young ladies called to see me the other day. One of the disadvantages of too much of the old yakity-yak is that people can soon tell when you don't know what you are talking about. As the old saying goes, even a fish wouldn't get caught if he'd keep his big mouth shut.

And the trouble is that when you write a column in a paper every week, discussing things of the countryside and the birds and the bees and this and that, and one thing and another and matters various, some folk tend to get the idea that you'd be a useful character to ask about hedgehogs. And what I know about hedgehogs you could put in a thimble and throw it away and not miss it.

In fact, in all my life I never ever remember reading anything about the love-life of the hedgehog. And when you come to think of it, this is in no way surprising, not by any manner of means. The hedgehog is a very prickly creature. And I wouldn't be surprised if there are more comfortable jobs in life than being a male hedgehog. So maybe there is no real love-life about it, and that is why nothing is ever written on the subject.

Well, the story these young ladies tell me is that one

evening recently they were in the house when the dog started barking outside and raising quite a shindig in one way and another. So they went out and there was this dear little hedgehog all curled up and out of harm's way.

Being kind-hearted, they put the dog in out of the way and got a saucerful of milk and the hedgehog immediately uncurled and drank it up in a manner which suggested that it was most welcome and acceptable, and then he trotted away.

Next night, like Abou Ben Adhem's angel, he came again, so the young ladies gave him another saucerful of milk which he drank up and away to go. Then, one night as he was crossing the road in search of his milk, there was a car coming along the road and it stopped, rather than run over the hedgehog, and the driver got out and picked up the hedgehog and put it in the boot and drove off.

Now the young ladies observed all this from an upstairs window because they were watching and waiting, and the hedgehog had been whisked away before they could do anything about it. But they did not mind when they came to think it over, because they thought this motorist was probably going to put him in his garden to keep the slugs down, and so he would be able to live happy ever after without getting run over.

And they asked me did I not think that this was so, and was it not a good thing that the hedgehog was thus taken away to a place of safety wherein to live happy ever after. And not being any wiser than I ought to be, I wasn't content to say yes and leave it at that. I had to go on to say supposing it had been a mamma hedgehog, and she had some little baby hedgehogs somewhere, so then the young ladies wanted to know which way do hedgehogs breed, and how the hell should I know?

Indeed I'd go so far as to say it's an awkward and embarrassing old question for two young ladies to ask a bloke.

According to the book, hedgehogs have one litter in May or June, and another litter in August or September. So it looks as if they know what it's all about and that they seem to like the idea. Which just goes to show that one half the world doesn't know how the other half lives. And as long as the hedgehog knows all he needs to know, well then, what I reckon is that that's his business.

Welsh Farm News, 2 October 1965

A skein of geese in a darkling sky

Yesterday evening we 'went for a run' as the saying goes. No form of expression could possibly be more misleading because those who indulge in this practice of 'going for a run' are the slothful ones who always have a motor car as an appendage, couldn't run if they tried, and it would be much better for them if they did. However, we 'went for a run'.

Not very far, but far enough to take us to a river estuary where the mud gives way to golden sand, and where lines of white waves in the midst of calm waters discover hidden sand bars which, in the more adventurous days of sail, sent many a stricken vessel to her doom. We were, indeed, far enough from the haunts of man to have ample opportunity to think on these things, and to observe much of that which we all too frequently pass by in haste.

Across the bay the distant headland stood out sharp and clear and looked ominously close. It needed little country knowledge to know that it brought warning of heavy rain to come. For the moment, however, it was an evening both pleasant and rich with the bird life which is the heritage of such lonely places.

There was red in the sky to complete an artist's picture, although the sinking sun was too pale to promise anything better than was being presaged by the distant headland. Elsewhere, inland on moor and mountain, there has been a decline in the curlew population of recent years, and there are those who maintain, probably with some justification, that increasing numbers of foxes have been responsible.

Here, however, these lonely seeming birds were in profusion. It is doubtless apt enough to refer to their call as bubbling as they glide above the heather in the summer sunshine, but on the silent shore it can never be anything but weird and haunting.

The oystercatchers, too, were in great number. Orange-beaked and pink-legged, they have ever been great favourites of mine.

They tell me now, though, that there are too many sea-pies, and that they are a great threat to the cockle industry. It could be so. But I wonder what returns are like for cockle-pickers these days. Without going too deeply into the subject I'd say there was a chance that, unless they're being better rewarded than other primary producers we wot of, cockle-pickers could one day be at a premium. In that case we'll be relying on the oystercatchers by-and-by to save us from getting hip-deep in cockles.

Low over the water a flock of dunlin sported, twisting and turning as at the word of command, one moment brown and the next a flash of white. Way out, midstream, the wild duck settled for the night, whilst some of their fraternity were off for nocturnal gorging on the stubbles. Two distant shots in rapid succession made me hope, quite uncharitably I suppose, that they were a right and left and that the marksman had been no more successful with the second barrel than with the first which, having missed, made the second one necessary.

It was a sharp reminder that life for the wild creatures is often as cruel as death is sudden. Indeed they reckon hereabouts there are not nearly as many birds as in days gone by, because of the constant experimental bangs emerging from a nearby Government establishment which presumably owes its continued existence in aid of the gainfully unemployed to the creed that it is somehow sacred to create employment. I wonder how disciples of this gospel would be received if they walked in sometime with dirty boots on a kitchen floor fresh-scrubbed by an ever-loving spouse. Well, it makes work, doesn't it?

It was whilst these thoughts were being pondered on that a skein of geese came through a darkling sky. The sea was at the full and it was in fact difficult to know whether high tide was past or yet to come. Whence they came or whither they went I know not. But I know for sure that there can be nothing in nature more exciting than to hear their wild calls and the beating of their wings in the quiet, lonely places.

Because of the experimental bangs and booms they are not seen as frequently in these parts as they were in former times. In any case it is early in the season for them to be on the wing. The locals reckon that it's the sign of a hard winter because they nest 'up in the cold parts' and already they are being driven south.

It seems ominous to be talking of a hard winter when the harvest has not yet been safely gathered in. But when the signs are there to be read it is up to us to read them. Certainly today it is pouring with rain, which the signs last night abundantly foretold. If the geese in turn are telling the truth, well, at least it's some consolation to have been there when they came and to have seen them.

Welsh Farm News, 24 December 1965

Officialdom at its worst

At the time of writing, the news has just been joyfully received by a highly amused nation that Goldie is once again upon the wing, foot-loose and fancy-free and a source of great hilarity to one and all.

Escaped once again from London Zoo, the great golden eagle soars and swoops above the metropolis, and likewise sits and observes the antics of those below as they devise some new trickery in an attempt to lure him back once again into captivity.

Not least delighted are the photographers and newsmen, who see in all this a great diversion from the troubles and tribulations of mankind in such items as Rhodesia, Vietnam and all the other horrible threats to world peace. One bookmaker is reported to be laying odds on Goldie not being back in his cage by Christmas.

Letters again pour into the papers about cruelty and nature. Some folks even suggest that, as Goldie apparently likes his freedom so much he should be allowed to wander wither he wilt, if thou knowest what I meanest.

This reminds me that last time Goldie was on the razzle he swooped threateningly on a yapping small dog. If there's one thing in this life I can't abide it's yapping small dogs that can't be hushed, and for this splendid deed Goldie earned my wholehearted commendation.

How long, however, before such capers would arouse the wrath of the Canine Defence League and other such noble-minded causes and turn Goldie into a public enemy to be hunted and slaughtered? It's all such a problem when we come to think how little some folks know of the need for man to be waging constant war against certain predators if he's going to survive.

Not that I'm suggesting for one moment that Goldie is anything of a menace to mankind. It's just that those who offer gratuitous advice on how to recapture him, or propound on whether he should be recaptured at all, are those who know least about it and show how little so many people know about the so-called balance of nature and the place, if any, of certain predators or pests in the natural scheme of things.

The only problem Goldie really presents is to the poor red-faced nuts who allowed him to escape a second time and now have the embarrassing task of trying to recapture him in the spotlight of publicity attendant upon their efforts with Goldie's every move being faithfully recorded and photographed.

This is joyful. This is great. This is as it should be. This was ever thus, because authority is there to be derided and poked fun of and, where and when possible, to have a snook cocked at it. This is because authority is so often an ass and, since time began, has been doing so many stupid things.

Examples of the folly and inefficiency of officialdom are legion but, for other reasons, one example is, and always will be, better remembered than any of the others.

Long years ago officialdom decreed that the people should be counted, for which purpose they would need to be gathered together in one place. And that place was Bethlehem.

Officialdom, however, had made but inadequate provision for accommodating those who were to be counted, and had come great distances. And so it was that Joseph, a carpenter from Nazareth, with his young wife, Mary, found it necessary to spend the night in a stable amidst the beasts of the field. And during that memorable night Mary's baby was born, and they laid Him in the manger from which the cattle fed. And his name was Jesus.

It was long before the miracle of television, and the exploitation of the occasion as one when something or other would be a suitable present to give to him or her. We have long since forgotten nearly all about it, except to use it as a good excuse for a first-class binge and a blow-out.

It was, however, as the birth of a baby will ever be, cause for great rejoicing, and it brought with it a wonderful promise of peace on earth. Perhaps the promise hasn't yet materialised, because we've forgotten or ignored the first part of the angels' rejoicing which was 'Glory to God in the highest'.

Even if, as always, we remember these things all too little at this time, it is nevertheless because of them that I offer you once again the age-old wish of a Merry Christmas and look back in gratitude at so many blessings along the way.

Welsh Farm News, 15 January 1966

No time for spivs – even with two watches

Knowing how easy it is to break New Year resolutions and how short-lived they usually are, I suppose I can say that I've now reached an age when I no longer bother to make any. Experience has taught its own lesson, so why waste time and energy?

Therefore, I do not wish you to take any part of what I say this week as in any way suggesting that I have been making New Year resolutions about the subject. In fact, the bitterness had crept into my soul, and my mind had been made up some time previously long before the New Year hove into sight.

I wish to speak to you about hotel head porters and tipping of same. As far as I'm concerned, they can all look forward to the biggest non-tip of the year. Especially on this business of taxis. It is something which has built up over the years and that's what is meant by experience.

Occasionally when it is necessary for me to stay in the capital city of the Land of Our Fathers, I permit a fairly well-known penitentiary in that fair city to cater for my modest needs. Always, upon arrival, the porters were most attentive and helpful in accompanying me up in the lift with my meagre possessions and showing me to my bedroom. And always, on these occasions, although we know it is a pernicious system, the odd shillings changed hands. Whenever I remonstrated that I was a big badger well able to manage my own small case, I was firmly overruled. What delightful characters they all were.

Then, one day, I arrived there *en route* for London with two fairly heavy cases.

By the sort of coincidence which always seems to

happen to me, but not to other mortals, the lift was out of order. And what d'you know? There wasn't a porter to be found. Seeing that I was on the fourth floor, I thought maybe the porter could earn his tip this time. But even the receptionist had discovered that the lazy so-and-so's had all gone into hiding. In earlier years I had ignored these manifestations of spivery. But now, I began to set up a resistance. No money has changed hands since. The next rather glaring example came back in the summer when I had occasion to attend a meeting in the Metropolis and, on emerging from the hotel where it had been held, wished to avail myself of the services of a taxi-cab to get me from by here to by there.

I was, as I thought, in luck's way, because, at that very moment, a taxi drew up to deposit a 'fare', as they call them, right on the pavement where I stood – presumably because he wished to enter the hotel from which I had emerged.

The gold-braided major-domo held the door open and his hand out whilst saying over his shoulder to me 'Taxi, sir?'

So I said yes, and he said very well, he'd call one. So I said: 'But this taxi will do me very nicely, thank you.'

He insisted, however, that this would not do at all and, as this now empty taxi drove off and he hailed one from across the way, I asked him why.

So he said, well, this was the custom, and it was how he got his living. As the fresh taxi drew up and this character, to whom by now I had taken a dislike, opened the door for me, with the other hand held out, I said, 'Thank you very much, and I hope you live very well out of it.'

The last straw came during Smithfield Week, when, after the mid-day jollifications arranged by a well-known commercial firm at a famous hostelry, it was pouring with rain. Now, normally, there is no problem whatsoever about taxis on these occasions, because a very regal-looking gentleman in a tall hat with a sort of feather in it, stands under the awning and conjures them up as if by magic.

On this occasion, however, niet, dim, nothing, dam all. The rain, d'you see. Everybody clamouring for them. So I says to the obviously uninterested magician, 'Wot, no taxis?' And he says, very off-hand I thought, 'Not a hope, mate.' So, by way of taking the old Michael, I says: 'Lend me that hat then, boy, and let's see if I can get any luck.'

However, I can see there isn't much hope of getting him to part with his hat, so I say to the three characters who are with me to stay where they are whilst I set off in the rain to try my luck and, sure enough, after I walk for about five miles in the rain, I find a taxi and grab it!

And I say to the driver will he please to go first to this famous hostelry to collect my three friends and, as he pulls up, out steps old high-hat and opens the door whilst beckoning over his shoulder for someone to come forward, and holding out his other hand in the manner of his kind.

But, as I step out of the taxi, I say, 'You're out of luck, Buster. You've got to go and find your own today.'

I then go and call my friends, and as we climb into the taxi old high-hat stands there with his hand out because after all these years the position has more or less become a fixture with him.

We drive away and that is another lesson learned the hard way.

In future, when there are plenty of taxis about and I want one, I shall allow them the privilege of hailing one for me, because I know that when there are none to be had I shall have to go and look for my own. When I have been recognised as a tight one, and they leave me alone, that'll be fine, because then we can all be happy.

There is, as I say, no need for a New Year's resolution. It'll just come natural like. The iron has entered my soul, and from now on it will be as much as I can do to find it in my heart to give such characters the time, even if I have two watches.

Welsh Farm News, 5 February 1966

What a lot of good cheer there is to be sure

I wish to cheer you up this week and I am sure this will come as a great relief to one and all, because there is so much misery in the world that it's a good thing to be cheered up now and again.

After many years in the business, I know that all sorts of characters get very cheered up indeed when I write about something unusual. Even so, what I wish to write about this week is nothing more unusual than bad weather. It is bad weather to be sure. But to regular readers of this column, the weather will come as no surprise, because I told you all about it last September.

In fact, I wrote a little piece for you in very rustic vein indeed, and I told you all about how I had seen the wild geese high in the darkling sky, or something like that, at the set of sun. Mind you, I'm not sure what a darkling is, but I always think it sounds nice, and it is always a great thrill to see and hear the wild geese under such circumstances and in such places.

I remarked at the time, however, that it was much too early in the season for such things to be, and added the further information, free and for gratis, that it was reckoned hereabouts to be the sign of a hard winter, and that's how it has turned out. Mark you, I could have been right and I could have been wrong, and it so happens I was right and that is why I remind you of it now.

It is said with very large lumps of truth that when you are wrong there are always plenty of so-and-so's to remind you of it, but when you are right you have to remind the so-and-so's yourself. Therefore and wherefore I remind you that I warned you last September that we were going to have a hard winter.

However, I do not wish you to get the idea from this that I consider myself to be in any way an authority on the weather, otherwise when the time comes, if I am proved wrong, there will be somebody to remind me of the fact and to accuse me of having raised a lot of false hopes about the place.

What I wish to speak of is a very serious matter whatever, which I only hear tell of this week, and I consider it my duty to bring it to your notice straightaway. As a matter of fact, I am talking to somebody about theories such as the world cooling off since breaking away from the sun, and resulting in a gradually deteriorating climate. I also refer to the belief that we are moving into another Ice Age which is a most desperate and diabolical thought indeed.

However, I am now in a position to inform you that there is no reason to have any fears on this score. In fact, all the bad weather is due to nothing more serious than the world being tipped over to a certain extent. I don't know whether this accounts for beatniks, juvenile delinquency, masked robberies and general mayhem and bloody murder.

It could be that the world is just a little bit upside down. Like I said, I wouldn't know about this. All I know for sure is what I'm told, which is that the world is now tipped over in such a way that our bit of it is further away from the sun which is just our rotten bit of luck.

For that matter, I don't suppose the characters who are now facing the sun and getting many years of drought are very pleased about it either. Whichever way you look at it, it's a serious matter, likely to induce an outsize dose of the heebie-jeebies in the worrying types.

I recognise that getting the world back on an even keel is likely to prove something of a task, but I think the FUW ought to send somebody a memorandum about it. If they do, however, and nobody takes any more notice than they do of any other memoranda they send, there is no need to worry. You can all be of good cheer.

That is why I write this column this week. To cheer you up, like. Because I am assured that the world will be tipping back into place again in about fifty years' time, and then the weather will start to improve and there will be much talk of global warming. And I think that this is joyful news.

Where the wild geese will be then I haven't a clue. Maybe they'll still be westering, or, if they have any sense, they'll have cleared to hell out of it. Certainly I don't expect to be in a position to be able to say 'I told you so', or care if somebody is writing in to say the fool was wrong again.

And that thought in itself will be enough to cheer some folks up. So what a lot of good cheer there is, to be sure.

Welsh Farm News, 12 February 1966

I wish to write for you this week on the subject of efficiency and also service to the customer, because it is well-known to one and all that I am a great authority on such matters. I also wish to explain about a certain mackintosh.

The wise ones reckon that maybe I wanted to look like that nice Mr Harold Wilson. Some of them just want to take the old Michael and reckon that I wanted to look like the NAAS characters and live in hopes of a spot of promotion.

As a matter of fact, only a few days after I obtain this new mackintosh I call on a friend of mine, and his wife says he is across the fields at the hay-rick loading hay with the man. So I go across to see him, and as I approach he shouts a greeting and says, 'Good God, Benjamin, I've just been slandering you. Do you know,' he says, 'when I see you coming across the fields all dressed up like this I say here's another of these lazy, good-for-nothing so-and-so's wondering what the hell to do next. I am pleased to see you.'

But this is only a case of mistaken identity, and I do not wish to look like anybody, whether it be the nice Mr Wilson or the NAAS characters or anybody else. In fact all I want before this is a new mackintosh, and this happens to be the one I fancy and which I am now wearing because it is reckoned to be very good for keeping out the rain and also the wind and is, therefore, very suitable for poor badgers who cannot afford to buy two coats, one for each purpose.

So a week or two ago I go into this shop and explain my needs, and the man says he is very sorry he does not have one in at the moment, but when do I want it. And I say tomorrow, and he says not to worry he will get one down from Swansea. And he also says he knows my size but he will check, just in case, and he puts the tape round me and says yes that is right I will require a 46.

So the next day I am going to Cardiff and it is blowing like the clappers from the east and there are no brass monkeys to be seen because of the great amount of cold everywhere. In fact this all happens as long ago as early November, during that very cold spell – so you will see that I ask for the coat with the winter still to come and in plenty of time.

As I am going out Mrs Brock says am I not going to wear my overcoat and I say no, because I am picking up my new mackintosh like the nice Mr Wilson on the way, which will keep out the wind as good as an overcoat and also be very good in case it turns to rain or snow. And she knows better than to waste time arguing with the fool, as she affectionately calls him, but just looks disgusted and off I go.

When I arrive at the shop, however, there is considerable agitation because Swansea have made a great mistake and sent down a 42, but the man telephones them and they have one in to fit me, and I can call for it on my way to Cardiff and make sure to ask for Mr So-and-so. And although I have no wish to go through Swansea, I make a little detour and this is what I do.

When I reach Swansea I park the car and then have to walk a long way to this firm's big shop and everybody looks at me as if I am crazy, because it is such bitter weather and I do not have any coat on whatsoever. And I go straight in and ask for Mr So-and-so, and it turns out he is a stupid so-and-so at that.

Ah, yes, he says here is my size and will I try it on, but I say it is a 44 and I want a 46. So he explains that in this make, like the nice Mr Wilson wears, it is different, and 44 is my size. So I say please to show me a 46, and he admits that they do not have a 46 in the place, but will I try on the 44.

So I try it on and it is too small, and this Mr So-and-so says yes it is a beautiful fit, but by this time I am losing my patience and I tell him does he not hear what Santa Claus says to the turkey, which is to go and get stuffed. Furthermore I decide to be independent of this concern and buy myself such a coat as I require in Cardiff.

By the time I reach Cardiff all the shops are shut, so I stay the night, and next morning at 9 o'clock I nip out smartish wearing a very ancient kind of garment which is usually in the back of the car for putting under dirty sacks of this and that and one thing and another, and no doubt I look considerably disreputable.

Unfortunately, however, it has now come on a Wednesday and apparently if shops feel that way about things they do not bother to open on Wednesdays at all. Furthermore it is now raining, snowing, freezing and maybe thawing all at the same time, and these are very desperate weather conditions whatever, and I have no alternative but to go round in my disreputable garment.

Eventually, when I return, I go back to the shop where I start in the first place, and the man orders me a 46 direct from the makers, and after about another twenty 'phone calls and seventeen postcards, and only nine letters it arrives

With price review discussions now getting under way I hope the nation understands about these things, because if agriculture served them no better than some of these characters who fool themselves that they're in competitive business we'd all be in pretty poor shape indeed. Which explains all about efficiency and service to the customer as well as about a certain mackintosh.

Welsh Farm News, 23 July 1966

The Badgers on holiday at Butlin's

It has been established by ancient custom that whenever I go on holiday I write a few lines for you just to say how things are going. From which you will see that there is no rest for the weary or the wicked, and I thought that I'd get that in quick before some clot says how lucky I am to have a holiday.

Now, as you all know, my taste in such matters is some lonely island, and live it as rough as you like, as long as there is a large measure of peace and quiet away from the world's mad bustle and strife, with particular emphasis on a prominent absence of all forms of humanity. Judge for yourselves, therefore, what manner of brainstorm must have assailed me before I agreed to set off on this current crazy venture.

We are at Butlin's. Really and truly. No joking. We're at Butlin's. And this has been brought about because one small badger was convinced by the commercial 'plugs' on the idiot's lantern that Butlin's would really be a great place to have a holiday. And, as Mrs Brock said, what's the point of older badgers having small badgers if they're not willing to do something for them sometimes?

You can imagine with what fear and trepidation I approached this ordeal. Especially as those in whom I had confided had done nothing to allay my worst forebodings. However, I have not only survived, but retained what little sanity I have ever had, and hope to be spared to write for you for many a long day yet.

One small badger was told on the first day that he could enrol as a young Beaver if he wished. In some respects he takes after his old man and, fortunately, was too cunning a little b----r (abbreviation for quickness for badger, beaver or anything else you can think of) to be caught on this lark, and has contrived to have an excellent time on his own account.

I have no intention of writing about the cheerleaders, the good morning razzmatazz, and all the organised guff which has become synonymous with the very name of Butlin's, because it's all been done before *ad nauseam*. All I wanted was peace and quiet and, quite unbelievably, I found it. Very nice lounges and odd spots here and there amidst the rose trees. Most peaceful.

In fact, I think Sir Billy Butlin must be quite a tidy little chap at heart because he's got it all worked out very nicely in theory, and obviously has the right ideas, with consideration for the aged and the infirm, as well as all manner of attractions for the tiny tots and the teenagers. Articles on the regimentation have often been grossly exaggerated.

What you have to remember, however, is that there are something like ten thousand inmates incarcerated here, and there are two thousand staff to look after them. And two thousand staff in themselves require some looking after and keeping an eye on, because they're mostly seasonal workers, and what do you expect to get these days anyway?

Parkinson's Law also operates the same as anywhere else, and all a departmental manager needs in order to stay in his job is for somebody under him to be doing his job for him. The only thing any of them seem to have worked out to perfection is how to pass the buck and nobody seems to know anything.

Notices here and there suggest that Sir B. would be interested in a personal note with any suggestions. One humorous character has wisecracked that the best suggestion would be for Sir B. to take a holiday here himself, saying that if he got a knighthood for organising it all, then we ought to have a leather medal apiece for putting up with it.

This doesn't sound very kind to me, but I'm told that Sir B. does in fact visit all his holiday camps a few times every summer, and that, before he comes, word travels along the grapevine and everybody puts their best foot forward. To which I can only add that it is our bad luck he didn't come this week.

However, I digress, because I wanted to tell you about the food, with special reference to the toast. To put it in words of one syllable, which are not likely to give the wrong impression, the food is not good. Neither is it very appetising. But when two thousand mouths come to the feeding trough at the same time there are bound to be problems.

You have read a great deal lately about cotels and speed of throughput, but, believe me, brothers, when you've had a week on this lot you realise why people say the animals are bound to be better off in the traditional cow-shed with individual attention. What it says in the brochure about individual tables with your own personal waitress is not only a myth and a mirage. It is strictly the old phonus bolonus.

The most joyful moments are when some unfortunate waitress drops a dish whilst dashing and everybody cheers like mad. One evening one luckless little wench not only drops the whole bag of tricks, but slips in it and rolls in it as well for good measure. She has the biggest cheer of the lot.

Anyway, about the toast. I asked the waiter about this and he said oh, no, this can only be obtained on a doctor's certificate. So next morning, having had enough peace and quiet to go on with, I go down to the medical centre where a notice proclaims that a doctor will be in attendance from 10 a.m. to 11 a.m.

In front of me at the window marked 'Enquiries' is a

young male character, I think, of about twenty years of age, with long hair, tight trousers and winkle-picker shoes. He wants a prescription for a bottle of aspirins. From which you will see that Sir B. also has his problems.

When the lady in Enquiries has passed this young character on to the queue in the waiting room, she says to me, 'What's yours?' So I say, 'What's my what?' And she says, 'What's your trouble?' So I say, 'I haven't any trouble, miss. I've never felt better in all my life.'

'All right,' she says, taking a deep breath and starting again, 'what do you want?'

So I say, 'I'd like a bit of toast, please.'

'Oh,' she says, very patiently, I think, 'this is the first aid post. You'll get toast in the dining room.'

Still at my most simple-minded, I say, 'Ah well, that's what I thought, like, but they said to come over here and you'd fix it up. Mind you,' I add, 'I thought it sounded a bit funny, like, but they said definitely you could fix it up, and so I've come over here to enquire, like, and I wonder if I can have a bit of toast.'

Just then a very nice nurse comes along, and she is the sort of pleasant character to make me feel almost sorry I never have a real illness.

'Oh, Sister,' says the lady in Enquiries, 'there's a camper here says he'd like to have some toast.'

'So would I,' says Sister. 'I haven't seen any since I've been here.' To which I offer, 'You want to go and see a proper doctor, girl.' So then we all have a good laugh, and she says, 'Well now, are you on a diet?'

To which I reply, 'Well, not exactly, but I reckon it's a good chance to start.'

They say that nurses are no fools, and I think that this could well be so. Certainly this one recognises in no time at all that she has a right Charlie on her hands, and she gives me a certificate straight away to say, yes,

I definitely ought to have some toast.

When it comes time for the evening meal I ask the waiter can I please have some toast for breakfast in the morning, and he says oh, no, I will have to have a doctor's certificate, so I give him my document, and he says good gracious what is this? He never sees one before in his life. So he calls one of his mates across, and they go into a huddle whilst their waiting operations are suspended all round and about, which I suppose is why it is called waiting at table. Then one of them goes off, and a very nice lady in a smart uniform comes along and addresses me in a very civil and courteous manner. And since it says in the guff that we have single tables, because this can be taken as four tables pushed together, I speak to the campers on the adjoining tables so that they can place their orders, and I am very popular with one and all at breakfast time when a trolley comes in laden with very nice toast, but I only help myself to one slice on account of the beautiful nurse looking at me in such a way that she obviously thinks I should go on a diet, and this is repeated until the end of our week's sojourn.

You may think there is a great deal of foolishness attached to this business, and I think you could be right and all. But, even at that, I reckon it's a far better holiday than anything you could have at a seaside holiday resort in the ordinary way and, if anybody wants to start an argument, I'm willing to give you chapter and verse.

After all is said and done, it's meant to be a holiday for the masses. I'm not keen on being a mass myself but, any time you can put up with being a mass for a little short while, then you could do worse. At least, the farmers can be glad that they use plenty of milk and serve fresh cream when that sort of thing is on the go. They also use real butter, and the bakers could be on to a good thing if enough difficult characters keep asking for doctor's certificates for toast.

What's more, these places cost millions of pounds to build and equip. Now the news cometh that the bank rate goes up again, and the banks have to take a lot of money out of circulation. Hence the apocryphal story that Sir B. has just had a cheque bounced. Paid it out lately for the new camp at Barry, and it comes back marked 'Refer to drawer – insufficient funds'. So Sir B. marches down to the manager and says, 'What do you mean – insufficient funds?'

'Oh,' says the manager, 'not you – us.'

So that's all for this week, campers, apart from the fact that, according to the morning Hallelujah chorus, the sun always shines at Butlin's, which ought to make it a pretty good place for haymaking.

Until next week then, this is Uncle Ben saying, 'By – byee!'

Welsh Farm News, 13 August 1966

The day was overcast and the round of summer shows was beginning to take its toll. They are convivial occasions sometimes.

Yet another show was in progress and the gentleman might well have pondered on the way of life which could necessitate the forfeiting of yet another afternoon nap.

He had had his lunch. From the overcast skies the little rain drops began to fall. They turned to bigger drops and they fell much faster.

So he retired to the sanctuary of his motor car to ride out the fury of the storm. And he went to sleep. He slept well as is the way of those who have a clear conscience or no conscience at all.

Long after the shower had passed, one of the girls began to show signs of worrying and eventually said: 'Do you think there's anything the matter with Father?'

So one of the boys looked into the car and said: 'No, he always sleeps like that when he's snoring.'

Later in the day he was again enjoying the show, appraising here and offering a little criticism there.

Eventually, being a well-known steward at much bigger shows, he said: 'Now, come on boys, it's time for these stewards to be getting the Grand Parade going.'

So then they told this well-loved character that the Parade had taken place whilst certain people were believed to have been fast asleep.

They told him it was a pity, because it was so well organised that he might have picked up a few wrinkles.

They told him a lot of things and, as always, he took it all in good part.

And I think it will be a long, long time before he lives it down.

* * *

I have seen all sorts of dogs in my time. Big dogs, small dogs, long dogs, short dogs, fat dogs, thin dogs. Not to mention hot dogs, gay dogs, and even dirty dogs.

I have seen highly intelligent dogs, and dogs that are just plain stupid.

But never have I seen a dafter dog than one I encountered a few weeks ago as he chased swallows with a highly intelligent look on his face.

From dawn to dusk he followed this fatuous and unrewarding pastime.

And in a way, whilst not exactly trying to justify him, his owner, a well-known sheepdog handler, at least sought to excuse him.

'His mother,' says he, 'was the best bitch I ever had.'

'Is that really so?' says I.

'His father,' says he, 'was twice a National winner.'

'Is that really so?' says I.

'His grandfather,' says he, 'appeared in five International Trials and was three times a winner. International, mind you. Not National.'

'Look at that!' says I.

'That's really so,' says he, 'and he used to chase swallows all day just the same.'

'And I'll bet he never caught one either,' says I.

'No,' says he, 'he never caught one either.'

Welsh Farm News, 29 July 1967

I wish to give you fair warning that this column this week will be considered by one and all to be a great deal of foolishness, so maybe you'd better not waste your valuable time reading any further if that's the way you feel about things.

And as the very few friends who will defend this nonsense will say, that is the charm of the column. You never know what the old fool will be on about next. In any case it may not be considered as a matter of such great foolishness by any little bald-headed Welshmen who read this column, because some characters do not like being bald whatsoever, and just look at the price of toupees.

It all starts with a report in the paper about some bald-headed coot, who is working in one of these intensive poultry units somewhere, and then one day he finds that the hair on his head is starting to grow again, which makes it look as if this poultry manure must be pretty potent medicine and don't make any mistake about it.

Like I remember a bald-headed blacksmith many years ago who opens up shop in the morning, and the first thing he does after getting the fire going is to rub his coal-dirty hand over his head just to get acclimatized. Not that this has anything to do with the story, but I cannot imagine anybody rubbing poultry manure on their heads and neither can you.

However, a character I know also reads about this bald-headed coot in the poultry shed, and so he decides to experiment and sets the boys to collect some of the white tops off the turkey droppings. Well, it is just about this time that a gypsy calls at the farm, and this gypsy has a very fine head of black wavy hair as is often the case with these characters. They are like that.

And this character who is collecting the turkey droppings asks the gypsy what about it, and the gypsy says that the secret is fat from round a badger's kidneys. Well, although they reckon that badgers are dwindling in numbers, I merely wish to state that there are still a good many little bald-headed Welshmen about.

So this character says that he will give the gypsy a pound if only he will bring him some fat from round a badger's kidneys, and sure enough a few days later the gypsy turns up with some in a mint-sauce jar. But by this time this character collects some of the white tops off the turkey droppings, and he thinks it will surely be a pity to waste these now that they are collected.

So what does he do but mix the turkey droppings up in a paste with the fat from round the badger's kidneys, and he puts it all together in a jar and screws the lid on. Then he begins to think some more about this business, and before he can come to any decisions or conclusions, or think up any more bright ideas, he notices that little hairs are sprouting up in the jar. So he keeps an eye on this business and is greatly excited to see the jar becoming full of rich black hair, not quite as stiff as bristles on a farmyard broom, but certainly stiffer than somewhat. But by this time he is becoming just a bit worried and is afraid to take the lid off the jar in case all this powerful black stuff gets out and he can't get it back into the jar again.

Well, I wish to state that I do not yet wish to see this phenomenon for myself, but this character gives an open invitation for one and all to come and see it any time they so wish. And whilst I am prepared to find that this is some great hoax, or that this is just another leg-pull, I certainly regard it as my duty to draw your attention to it.

I think some journalists will be quite likely to agree

that this is a very good story indeed.

And, after all is said and done, we do not always lag behind. Not long ago, when other papers are content to use Ministry of Agriculture handouts about brucellosis and the need to take advantage of the wonderful free vaccination scheme, we were telling you something about the simple facts of life, including the uselessness of the S19 vaccine. And there were people who said that that was great foolishness as well.

I wonder what they have to say about it now.

Welsh Farm News, 6 May 1967

Story of the calf that went astray

I've explained to you before about us not being very efficient farmers, so it won't come as too much of a surprise for you to learn that rather odd things are apt to happen here from time to time.

But something happened here last week which was rather more remarkable than usual as well as being rather distressing. We had a cow calve on the Thursday afternoon. After milking at about seven o'clock in the evening, the calf was with her mother in the field having a real good bellyful of milk, very strong on his legs, except that it was a heifer calf, so that it was a case of being strong on her legs, but it is customary always to speak of a calf as him and his and so on when they are just small baby calves. And this was very much of a baby calf, because it was only born that afternoon. What's more the sun was shining and the birds were singing tweet-tweet in a most merry fashion in the woodland glade. It was a very peaceful and rural scene to be sure.

I am led to believe that at such a time of year, on some very efficient and well-managed farms, it is quite customary and normal good husbandry practice to leave the cow and calf together, so why should we be any different? So this is what we did, and that's how it happened as I shall now relate.

On the Friday morning, which is to say the next day on account of Friday coming after Thursday in these parts, the calf was gone. The cow was just kicking up a fuss and looking anxious in the spot near the bottom of the field where she had calved. So maybe in fairness to the cow I'd better explain a few more of the details.

At the bottom of the field there is a wood. There was

also at the time of this occurrence an electric fence there. It was obvious that the calf could have walked under the fence into the wood and that the cow would have been unable to follow. And this was a reasonable deduction from the fact that the calf was nowhere to be seen, and the cow was cutting quite a caper and considerably distressed about the whole business.

I mention these points because it is well-known how a cow will hide her calf and march away occasionally to feed it and keep an eye on it. And when the silly old moo is playing it crafty these hidden calves can sometimes be the devil to find. I've had some of it in my time and can usually recognise the symptoms. But this wasn't one of those cases at all. The calf had apparently wandered off and had certainly disappeared.

All day Friday the search went on, and we continued at odd times to carry on searching until the shadows lengthened into twilight, and the merry songs of the little dicky-birds going tweet-tweet in the woodland glade were hushed and stilled. There was never a sign or sound of the lost calf, but we had a bit of luck in one other way.

Somebody had been in the wood cutting beansticks and, as they had cut a very big bundle indeed, they had left them there with a view no doubt to collecting them on some suitable vehicle some dark and quiet evening. But I couldn't for the life of me remember anybody having asked me could they cut some beansticks, so I took the old-fashioned view that maybe my claim to the beansticks was as good as theirs. I carried them home anyway.

I figured that if they'd been cut by somebody local who knew he was welcome, he'd be happy enough to come a-knocking at the door and tell me I'd had his beansticks. But I thought that, if they'd been cut by somebody else, then what-the-hell. And a couple of beansticks are always handy in the old garden in case anybody ever gets round to digging it. All that has nothing to do with the calf, but I mention it just to show that there's never a dull moment.

We had a look at odd times again on the Saturday but we didn't get any joy out of it. The generally accepted idea was that it was the foxes. One suggestion was that it could have been a two-legged fox the same as was after the beansticks, but I didn't go much on that idea myself.

However, that's the way it goes. They reckon that where you have livestock you're also bound to have dead-stock. So we reconciled ourselves to our loss and you get over things eventually.

It was a very nice surprise therefore to see this little customer wandering round the field on the following Tuesday morning and looking quite perky, but just a trifle empty and obviously hungry.

So, if my reckoning is right, that's four days and five nights, which is a long time for a baby calf to be alone and hungry in a cruel world. But I know that somebody is sure to turn up and say that they once have a calf which could beat that by a considerable margin. And it would be interesting to hear of such incidents.

It's only fair for me to warn you, though, that since this happened, folks have been telling me of some spectacular outings to be sure. Already there's been the story of one that turned up after eight days.

Any advance on eight?

Welsh Farm News, 16 September 1967

À propos nothing at all very much, which is as good a
way as any other to start off a weekly contribution, and
happens to be a change from 'Like I said', I thought you
might like to hear about some geese about which I am
reading recently, which maybe sounds awkward but is
good grammar.

And talking about being awkward, it is only fair to
point out that geese look very awkward at the best of
times, as this particular article points out, saying that
they always look to be in danger of tipping forward on
their faces, or back on whatever it is they call them, and
still be polite in a newspaper column which some
people read and are only too pleased to say why do
they allow him to say such things.

With geese generally being such unstable-looking
characters, it is not surprising to hear tell that, when
they have looked on the wine when it is red, they
become very unstable characters indeed, and in fact
these geese become more unstable than somewhat.
They are out for the count and are very drunk geese,
and it is altogether a very sad story.

The way of this occurrence is as follows, and it
happens out in Germany where a good dame is making
a very tasty brew of cherry brandy, and it is well known
to one and all that a drop of the old home-brewed has
a considerably powerful kick in it. In fact, Mrs Brock
makes some ginger beer for haymaking this year and
even that blows the cork half-an-inch into the ceiling
plaster, and we reckon we do well to keep the ginger
beer in the kitchen, let alone in the bottle.

However, when the good dame in Germany is half-
way through the operation, she finds that the fruit is
sour, so she throws it out to the geese, and you can
guess the rest, because I remember once I tell you what

happens when we feed the dregs from the casks of the raisin wine to a couple of pigs that are just about fit to kill. They are drunk for a fortnight, and we do not kill them for a long time after that.

So what with one thing and another it is not surprising that the geese get very drunk indeed and start plaiting their legs every which way, and it is a fact known to one and all that geese are not such well-balanced creatures as to be able to indulge in such cavortings for very long, and in no time at all they look like very gone goslings indeed. In fact they are out for the count, and it is a very long count at that.

Well, naturally, the good dame becomes very worried to behold such a sad sight, but never gives the cherry brandy a thought, so she calls in her neighbours, who are full of wisdom and good advice, as such characters usually are, and they all agree that the geese have been poisoned and will not on any account be fit to eat. But they think the feathers will be all right, and it will be a pity to waste the feathers, so they all give a hand and set to with the good dame, until the geese and the gander are feathered in a most workmanlike manner and very tidy to be sure.

Now most stories have an ending that is either sad or happy, but I'm blessed if I can think which this one is, because next morning, when the dame comes down, she can hear a lot of familiar honking outside her cottage door, and when she opens up there are her geese shaking off their hangover and on their feet to a certain extent, but looking very cold and miserable on a frosty morning, like Maharishi Yogi coming back from a happening without either his flowers or his face fungus.

Now, like I've said before, everybody knows what to do about a feathered goose except the poor so-and-so who has a dozen of them.

So the good dame goes off again to fetch her neighbours, but they turn out to be not nearly as full of advice and good ideas as the day before. They recognise the difficulty of sticking the feathers back on again, and the impossibility in any case of finding which feathers belong to which goose. Finally they go off arguing amongst themselves and leave the good dame getting the geese in by the fire to save them catching their deaths from cold, and making some flannel jackets for them to keep warm until some more feathers can grow.

There is a moral in this story which is very plain. Because the paper in which I am reading about these inebriated geese is way back in 1881, which is a long time ago, and I am looking for something else at the time. But to go looking through old papers is fatal, because your attention wanders all over the place. And what I always say is that, if you're going to go delving into old newspapers, you want to have plenty of time on your hands and don't make any mistake about it at that.

Welsh Farm News, 16 December 1967

Now as it was written this was a time of great trouble and the shepherds and humble men who tilled the soil were sore afflicted. And even the trouble that was known as Little Harold was forgotten for a time, and the greatest of their troubles at this time was called foot-and-mouth, which was the greatest of such troubles for many moons. And the cattle and the sheep and the little hisso pigs were slaughtered and pits were digged, and the cattle and the sheep and the little hisso pigs were buried therein.

Now such was the virulence of the disease that was known as foot-and-mouth that great was the concern throughout the land, wherefore was it incumbent on all men that they should do no manner of thing which would spread the disease from one place to another place. And thus it came to pass that word went through the land that none should call on the places where dwelt the shepherds and humble men, nor should the shepherds and humble men gather together in one place.

Now some there were at times such as these who spake in parables to their fellows. And the parable they spake at this time was of the wind, and they spake now saying that withersoever the place from which the wind bloweth, and no matter what evil it bring, surely would it bring good for some men no matter in what place the wind bloweth to them withersoever they might be, for were it not to blow some good it were an ill wind indeed.

And the shepherds and humble men thought on this parable and they saw that it was good.

For there were in the land at this time many that were called Nass, and forget not the first letter at all times lest they be confused with the donkey that is without understanding. And those that were called Nass would gather the shepherds and humble men together into one place that they might speak unto them of fertiliser, which was known as ferts and manure and other words besides, and speak also of efficiency and many wond'rous things.

And those who sold the ferts for many pieces of silver rubbed their hands and were joyful. And so great was their joy that they themselves would even gather the shepherds and humble men together into one place to speak to them of ferts and give them bread and wine that they might come unto these places even if they cared not to hear about these ferts. And some there were who received their pieces of silver for the fodder for the cattle which they sold to the shepherds and humble men. And likewise would they also gather the shepherds and humble men into one place to speak to them of the wond'rous things and likewise efficiency. And the shepherds and humble men would speak together and say surely this is better bread and wine than when we go to hear those who speak of the ferts.

And the places whereunto the shepherds and humble men were gathered for this purpose were very cold and draughty places, and no man would go to them unless it be for the bread and wine or to hear his own voice, or in case he would not hear something which he would like to hear, especially if his neighbour should be there to speak of other neighbours, and always it was the same shepherds and humble men who were seen in such places. But now that word had gone throughout the land, no manner of men were gathered together unto such places, and those that were called the Nass were sore troubled because they had many things to teach the ignorant shepherds and humble men, especially about efficiency, and now they could not teach them.

And those there were who spake of efficiency, who would draw nigh unto the dwellings wherein dwelt the shepherds and humble men. But word had gone through the land and they came not.

And there were those who wished to sell the ferts for many pieces of silver and they came not.

And likewise there were those who wished to sell the fodder for many pieces of silver and they came not.

And there were those who had sold the ferts and the fodder for many pieces of silver in former times who would say can'st thou not give us something on account. And they came not.

And there were those who would call for pieces of silver to ensure that that which might happen could not happen but, if it did happen, it would be known as insurance. And they came not.

And those who drew nigh to collect the pieces of silver for the insurance also wished for twice as many pieces of silver for the Union which was called increased subscription. But they came not. And there were many others besides. And they came not.

And the shepherds and humble men were without stint and were joyful. And notwithstanding all the troubles they had seen before their eyes, and notwithstanding that they had themselves suffered, there came to them no remembrance either of that or of any sorrow in the world. And they were not aware of having ever spent a time more joyous and delightful than that.

And the shepherds and humble men considered not the efficiency, but concerned themselves with their many tasks without let or hindrance and did all that it was meet and right that they should do.

And this was a good thing.

Welsh Farm News, 15 June 1968

Danger vipers

Dr O.F. Conran, who farms at Tycanol, near Brynberian in the foothills of the Preseli mountains in north Pembrokeshire, has become a man with a mission.

The story of how he gave up his medical career after some years working in Africa has already been told in *Farm News*. But, although he farms in a lonely spot, and has fitted in happily amongst the small local community, he has not entirely forgotten the needs and problems of the outside world.

And one of their needs, although they cannot always see it, is to be saved from themselves.

The trouble is that so much has been and is being done to attract townspeople into the countryside and to throw everything open to them, while nobody has done anything to warn them of the dangers inherent in setting foot on untrodden paths.

Admittedly there have been all sorts of fatuous campaigns, asking people to shut gates after them and not to deposit litter and all that sort of twaddle, but this is merely to appeal to their better nature. The law is also very unhelpful on the subject. They have to be caught in the act, and this means devoting a life-time to sitting and watching, which is a non-starter. It just can't be done.

Time was when a notice about a bull was a help, and the presence of a bull in a field could often work wonders. But authority in its blighted folly has pretty well put a stop to all that in its attempts to lure the unsuspecting into even worse dangers. New laws on the subject will be even more stringent.

To put up a notice saying, 'Beware of the Bull' is to imply that the bull is dangerous and to invoke the rejoinder that it should therefore be kept under control. And just you try to persuade anybody that it is perhaps even more dangerous to go into a field where a fresh-calved cow has her calf with her.

Signs about dogs are also on a par with signs about bulls. Just a joke. And ill-tempered dogs, like fractious bulls, must be kept under control. There's a law about it.

Would any townsman ever think of asking before venturing into a field whether the ram was nasty? Yet they could give any pampered child a nasty old clout.

Dr Conran has all these creatures. Bulls, cows with calves at heel, rams, dogs and geese. They can be very nasty, too. He also has mountain ponies and a stallion. Does anybody need to be told that a stallion will kick? Yet what do townspeople do? Some treasure, fresh come from watching a television programme on Survival, will as likely as not go up to it and offer it a crust of bread.

Dr Conran does not object to visitors leaving his gates open and trampling down his fences, even in fields where there is no footpath. What is the use of objecting anyway? But he worries terribly in case they should run into personal danger.

So, even though they are prepared to run the gauntlet of these more evident dangers, there is still the lurking menace of which people must be warned.

Like the vipers. Poisonous they are. And very painful. And you just never know where they might be lurking underfoot waiting to strike. Not that anyone is suggesting for one moment that the vipers are so thick that you can't put a foot between them. But you don't need that many to do the damage. You only need one bite from a viper and that's it and all about it.

So Dr Conran, a public-spirited man for all his desire to live quietly in the countryside, has put up notices at strategic points saying about the vipers. Red letters on a white background. Very effective.

Well, he can't be expected to keep the vipers under control, can he? Not like the bulls and the rams and geese and that. There's no law about vipers.

There was a belief once held that the vipers of the Preseli range were distant relatives of the deadly gaboon vipers, but it would probably be necessary to take a blood test from someone who'd been bitten by one to know for sure.

One of the biggest problems is that, should anyone be bitten by a viper, there's no serum nearer than Cardiff – which is a long journey from Preseli, with the roads what they are, and the railways nearly all closed down. Perhaps the victim could telephone the Welsh Holiday and Tourist Board for advice. Or better still, perhaps the Board could issue a pamphlet on the subject. Except that it isn't as easy as it sounds.

Dr A.T.T. Forester, a snake-bite authority who was on leave from Nairobi and spending a short holiday with Dr Conran recently, told me: 'More damage is often done by the first-aid workers than the snakes.'

Mrs Conran, related (a sort of cousin) to the remarkable Snake Man himself, C.J.P. Ionides, also emphasised the difficulties of trying to treat a snake-bite in such a remote area. Dr Forester also volunteered the information that even more people die in Africa from bee stings than from vipers. So maybe farmers who have bees ought to give some thought as to whether they should put up some notices saying: 'Beware of the bee.'

Where there are both, the notice might say: 'Beware of the bee vipers.' Or is that too obvious?

There only remains, therefore, the question of being helpful to the trippers who wish to cross that land where there happens to be a footpath, and where the vipers are possibly not as numerous.

'This is quite simple' explained Dr Conran. 'You just paint arrows saying, "The path is here", and they're like a chicken which will follow a white line once you've put its nose on it.'

But, remember, there's always the danger that some misguided enthusiast might paint the arrows to lead to a terrible snake-pit. And if that were to happen it would be found that the sting isn't always in the tail.

Welsh Farm News, 22 June 1968

This is not a script for a music-hall comedian. To start with, there's probably nothing funny in it anyway. I can only give you my honest assurance that it is a faithful record as far as I can remember of a one-way conversation to which I had to listen a few days ago.

It was in that first fine flourish of hay-fever weather, and I had to call on the agents for a well-known make of mowing machine because we wanted one little part. Just a little part. Nothing complicated fortunately. Just a little one.

There was but one character apparently in charge of the 'Spares' department, and he was engaged upon the telephone.

How long it had been going on I don't know, but from the time when I came upon the scene, his part of the conversation went like this:

'Which wheel is it then? Is it the big one or the small one? . . . The small one. Well, what bearings have it got? There's two sorts like. Is it ball-bearings or a ball-race?

No, well it all depends see. If it's ball-bearings then you've got the one with th'other thread on it. Hold on a bit . . . Here 'tis . . . It's the same model but a different number. No, it don't show it here but have a look. What type of nut have you got? . . .

Hello. The same size? Hold on a bit then . . . it looks as if you've got the one with the longer rod on it . . . Have a look then . . . Hello. No, well the thread's the same, but the nuts is a bit different, and if you don't get the two workin' together you'll have the . . . Hold on a bit . . . Hello. Here 'tis. I got it. No, but it all depends, see. There's two types of bearings on them as well like. There's ball-bearings, and then some got the conical bearings. Hold on . . . no they don't show it here. Have you got the . . . hold on a bit.'

This bit of nonsense had taken between ten and fifteen minutes to enact. At this stage he gave the unknown sufferer at the other end of the telephone a brief respite from his torment and came to attend to me. By now a mechanic from the service department had joined me along with two other farmers. Patient looking characters. And I reckon they needed to be.

Fair play to the stores-type, he knew what I wanted and marched off to get it. Then he went back to the telephone.

So I said to the service mechanic, 'Is it always like this here?'

And he looks at me and he says, 'Good God, this is nothin'. A couple of days of this weather and there'll be a queue all down the passage and right down the lane there.'

So much for this weather. And three cheers for the 'Spares' department.

Welsh Farm News, 13 July 1968

So you want to know about the tourist trade and hotels and efficiency and that. You know all about being more efficient, because that's what farmers are constantly being told they have to be.

And farmers are also constantly being told to put out the welcome mat for the summer visitors, so I'll give you my version of the affair because you always express such a keen interest in my travels, and I know there's nothing you like better than a good laugh at my expense.

Well, there I was travelling through mid-Wales one evening, and I stopped at a market town which shall be nameless except to mention as the saying goes that it is not a hundred miles from Dolgelly what was, but is now Dolgellau or something like that.

I called at a hostelry where I stayed some dozen years ago, and where on that occasion I was treated rather well. That's why I called there this time. These places change hands over the years, I suppose, but sometimes this even results in an improvement. It isn't always a change for the worse.

A gentleman, who could have been the manager for all I know, emerged from the little office behind the reception desk to tell me yes, I could book a room for the night and here's the key – 'You can find your way up all right. It's on the second floor.'

I'm an old badger. I grant you that. If I see some poor underfed porter type struggling with my case I'm the first to take it off him. But I just don't like being told at these places that I have to carry my own case. Take it or leave it sort of thing. Even so, I was tired and didn't feel like answering back.

'Of course,' said this character, 'you're too late for anything to eat.' Well, it was then 8.40 p.m. and what's all this nonsense about catering for the tourists anyway?

'Oh, that's all right' says I, 'perhaps you can fix me a ham sandwich and a glass of milk maybe.'

No, he couldn't do that – 'But I'll tell you what. Just go round to the hotel next door. They'll feed you. They go on serving later than we do.'

So I did that, and had a real nosh-up and was waited on by a young chap who looked as if he was keen to make me feel welcome. It struck me that I should have booked in at that hotel in the first place, and I'll be wiser next time.

Next morning I bought a couple of papers and a paper-back novel which caught my eye at the newsagent's nearby, and reported to the dining room for breakfast at 8.35 a.m. The 'house rules' stated that breakfast would be served from 8.30 a.m. to 9.30 a.m. and, as I had an appointment about twenty-five miles away at 10 a.m., I thought that would be just about right. Poor fool. Poor blighted fool.

The waitress showed me to a table. Five minutes later she asked me to move. After another five minutes she moved me once more. This time I finished up facing the debris left behind by someone who had been at the trough before me. There were plenty of other tables freshly laid, but never mind, eh. I'm like that. Don't you worry, girl. We've all got our problems.

I read the first paper, and I read the second paper. But I failed to catch the eye of the apparently harassed waitress. So it was a toss-up whether to start on the paper-back novel or call it a day and maybe make life slightly easier for her. As it was now 9.05 a.m. and there were people leaving the dining room who had had their breakfasts, whilst I, who had been in there before them, hadn't even had my order taken, I decided to ease her burden and just went out and asked for my bill for bed and morning tea. No, not breakfast. Just bed, and no breakfast, for which I'd waited for half an hour without any luck. Well, that was a problem. They'd never known anything like that before. So I said, come to think of it, I'd never previously waited half an hour for breakfast without getting it, but I couldn't see that it signified. So there was an impasse, if you know what I mean, until I had a thoroughly bright idea and said let's ask the manager. But it was still not quarter past nine and he wasn't down. So I left my name and address and said to send me a bill when they'd worked it out. Highly irregular, but I thought it was a safer and wiser course of action than settling in full and then writing to the manager, when he was out of bed, to ask for a rebate.

Now I await results and am wondering whether I shall also be expected to contribute the ten percent service charge. Nice point it will be. Very interesting. What service?

Mark you, there are plenty of folks who will say that I could do with missing a meal now and again, and I would be inclined to agree with them. But I can think of cheaper and less annoying ways of doing it, and even a badger has to refuel sometimes.

But don't talk to me about encouraging the tourist trade, or about farmers becoming more efficient. That would really be the last straw to break the poor old badger's back.

Welsh Farm News, 2 November 1968

A matter of convenience

There's one thing about it, anyway. Whatever they say about the lavatory facilities at the Royal Welsh they are at least open for the convenience of those who want to use them.

That is to say, as long as somebody can find the key and remembers to open them in the first place. And the poor old Royal Welsh is picked on often enough, so how about picking on somebody else for a change? Like the Dairy Show, for example, which is held at Olympia.

A very nice place they have for the gentlemen of the Press there. Right down in the bowels of the earth it is, with lavatories nearby, and running water and all. All marble what-nots and mirrors all over the place, and a hook on which to hang your jacket. Most thoughtful.

Until the day when the Royal personage was due to visit the show. The Duke of Kent it was. Nice little chap they say. In fact, come to think of it, maybe our Royal family must be pretty terrific characters to remain as popular as they do in spite of the congenital idiots and fawning morons by whom they are surrounded.

I'm quite sure it wouldn't have been anything to do with the young Duke but, because he was likely to want to use this particular marble hall about lunchtime, it had to be closed for the entire morning. The gentlemen of the Press had to climb the long flight of stairs and go elsewhere in search of the answer to their most pressing needs.

I know there's a so-called lift service, but half the time you press the bell in vain when you wish to avail yourself of it, and they're operated anyway by the communistic types who shut the door in your face when they see you hurrying towards them.

On one occasion I caught one of them in an unguarded moment as I thought, and asked him did they never come in answer to the bell. And he said, oh no, they were having to stand by for the Duke. So, what with one thing and another, you might just as well use the long flight of stairs in the first place. And if you think that's funny, mates, then you try it when you've left it to the last minute in the fond and foolish belief that all you need to do is nip across to the other side of the passage.

Well, as everybody knows, they have press conferences at Olympia, the same as at all the well-run functions, and one character, who shall be nameless, but you can make a rough guess if you want to, ups and says what about it? And does it mean that there's something wrong with the Duke, or that the gentlemen of the Press are some sort of social pariahs?

Well, they wouldn't dare answer yes to either part of such a question as this, and so the President and all the big badges around him shake their heads and say this sounds like a most foolish business as far as they can make out, and they do not seem to know anything about it, but it will certainly be looked into.

Next year I propose to follow this matter a little further. If there is a next year that is. Because it seems for sure that, whatever the future of the Dairy Show might be, it's not going to be at Olympia for much longer. And can you wonder?

On the same day that I was in ill-humour over the lavatory nonsense I stopped by a place of refreshment and bought a couple of hamburgers or whatever, as they call them – a bun with a bit of meat and some onions in it. I didn't object to paying two shillings and threepence for these morsels, because I'm not by nature the complaining type. But you can accept my word for it that I blew my top when I asked for a glass of milk to go with them and was told I couldn't have it.

They couldn't spare it. They just had enough for the tea and coffee. And this, mark you, at the Dairy Show in a land which is swimming in milk. And it wasn't a shortage caused by the excessive demands of vast crowds of people, because the attendance is falling every year.

Oh yes, I know. Milk is available in certain appointed places. But I didn't want it at the appointed place. I wanted it where I was having the buns with the bit of meat and the onions at two shillings and threepence apiece. And that wasn't possible because Lyons hold the controlling share at Olympia, and since they are the caterers, whatever they say is law. And if they don't choose to sell milk by the glass the long-suffering customer can go elsewhere. Which is what the Dairy Show will soon be faced with having to do. And, when they go, I hope they'll go somewhere where nobody has any monopolies.

Once upon a time I wrote on these lines with a warning when it looked as if certain brewery characters showed signs of wanting to buy their way into the Royal Welsh. That pitfall was avoided but we might yet learn to everybody's benefit that all men, even if not equal, are all human, even Dukes and the *crachach*, and likewise anybody else who is likely to stop and ask you could you tell them where it is please.

Welsh Farm News, 15 March 1969

Years and years ago there was a book in school in which there was a story called The Last French Lesson. The scene must have been set in Alsace Lorraine and had to do with the German occupation and the fact that there would be no more teaching of French. It was all very sad.

The thought of it comes back to me now only because there is to be no more *Farm News,* and this is therefore the last column I shall be writing for you. And that makes me very sad – apart from the money. When I was in at the birth, and this column was launched upon an unsuspecting, and doubtlessly ungrateful nation, I didn't give any thought to the possibility that I might also be in at the death.

There were such great ideas and such fond hopes. Of such stuff dreams are made. We were to be ensuring a free flow of information amongst farmers, and I don't know what-all, as the saying goes. Certainly it was being hailed as a great service to Welsh agriculture, and I believed then, as I believe now, that there was and still is a place for such a paper.

Perhaps one day some enthusiastic lover of everything Welsh may decide to write the story of the paper's existence, and the vicissitudes with which it was beset.

When they do, I hope they will ask me to fill them in on the background. I reckon I could tell them a thing or two and I won't put it no higher.

But what's the good of bothering about that now? It's just so much water under the bridge, and who cares?

Many is the time when I have nearly been doing my nut to find a subject for the week's offering. Once I missed through illness, but otherwise was able to keep up the flow, always out to oblige the customers.

Or, as the farmer said to the land-girl, 'We had a lot of fun, no harm done, and thanks for the memory.'

Now that this moment has arrived, however, I realise how much I shall miss not having to sit down once a week and wait for the muse to take over. Very often I just got a hell of a kick out of it anyway.

Always, I am glad to say, I deeply appreciated the privilege of having such a platform from which I could regularly hold forth and air my views on subjects various. I know I annoyed a good many people, and was never conscious of trying very hard not to, but equally, I know that I made many friends whom I would never otherwise have been able to meet.

Some of these have been faithful readers and supporters ever since the paper started. As I did, they rejoiced when the paper acquitted itself well, and were saddened whenever it took wrong turnings. It is on their account that I feel most sorry, because they will be missing something which they always felt was worthwhile.

However, that's life and how it goes. It is something I would not have missed for anything, and they are years on which I shall look back with much pleasure.

So cheerio for now.

Modern Farmer, December 1974

The infallible mousetrap

There are, so they say, more ways of killing a cat than stuffing it with cream. This fact has long been known to one and all.

However, I do not wish to say anything about the cat. On this occasion I wish to say something about the mouse. In the plural at that, which amounts to mice all over the place, and about how I hear tell that it is not necessary by any manner or means to have a cat in order to catch a mouse. In fact, having a cat to catch a mouse can amount to diabolical cruelty, according to some folks.

Now this character who explains to me about getting rid of the mice is such a tender-hearted character that he will not think of turning a wicked great cat on to a defenceless little mouse. But he is not such an affluent character that he can allow the mice to go on raiding his larder, so I say the best way to stop them is to cement their holes up, but he says he couldn't find anybody to hold them, and I say that is not what I mean.

This character, however, says they have claws like pneumatic drills. He also says do I ever see a mouse in a trap and do I notice what nice eyes they have?

To be sure I once see a mouse in a trap and the wire has caught him slap-dab across the nostril which is now considerably flattened, and I happen to notice at the time that his eyes seem to be looking up in a very surprised manner indeed. So I am able to state that yes, their eyes are very expressive.

Well, this character sits there one night by the fireside thinking of this and that and one thing and another, and he recalls a time when he is very young and catches birds with a riddle, with some crumbs under it and a bit of stick to hold it up, and some cotton to pull the stick away when the birds are underneath it, most unsuspecting.

And before you can say mouse-in-the-flour-sack, what does he do but put down an empty inverted tobacco-tin, with a match-stick to prop it up, and shoves the other end of the match-stick into a bit of cheese and sits there and waits. As he explains, he puts the match-stick end of the tin and the bit of cheese against the wall, so that the mouse has to attack it with his body under the tin, and he just sits there, and in no time at all away goes the match-stick, bang goes the tobacco-tin, and there's the mouse catched, and I am quite sure his eyes must show him to be a very surprised mouse indeed, but this character cannot see this for himself at the moment because the mouse is charging around like an agitated tortoise and hurling the tin every which way.

This character states it is what you might call a most singular performance and more amusing than somewhat.

Next thing he does is slide a bit of paper under the tin, then he raises it very gently and catches the mouse by the tail. It is when he holds the mouse up by the tail that he notices what nice little eyes it has, and he doesn't know what to do with the mouse, because he doesn't feel like killing it, and he reckons the world is a big old place altogether, with plenty of room for the odd mouse or two as well as himself.

And his wife says no, indeed, he must not even think of killing it. She is also very tender-hearted. Well, this character cannot stand there holding a mouse by the tail all night, no matter how expressive his little eyes are, and so he puts him outside and continues catching mice under the tin, and they all have expressive little eyes, and so he puts them all outside.

What's more, he is no mug at that, because he considers the possibility of the mice coming back into the house, and so he puts a little dab of white paint on each one, but he does not catch any mouse with a dab of white paint on it, so he knows he does not catch the same mouse a second time.

Personally I do not think any mouse in his right mind will wish to come within ten thousand miles of such a contraption a second time, but I do not make any reference to such. All I say is that the owls must be having a high old time of it round this place, and he says well, they have to live as well, don't they, and what about the balance of nature then?

So I say yes, indeed, I hadn't thought about the balance of nature. But then, I wouldn't have thought about an inverted tobacco tin in the first place.

Modern Farmer, Volume 12 Number 5, 1974

The last time I wrote a little piece for you in these pages I made some passing reference to the recent general election.

Without pretending to know anything of the finer points which distinguish between reclamation and speculation, I seem to recall that in the confusion of the run-up, when every hopeful candidate clutched at every passing straw which seemed likely to yield a vote, there was some talk here and there about the selfish types who had two houses – one in which to live, and one to which they could repair for holidays, and there is no law against this. Not as yet, anyway.

Now it is a fact well-known to one and all, among country people at any rate, that whenever a country cottage comes on to the market, even if nobody has lived in it for the last ten thousand years, there is always somebody from London or Birmingham or somewhere like that to snap it up at a price which genuine locals wouldn't dream of paying, even if they wanted it in order to live in it themselves, which obviously they don't, otherwise why didn't they buy it years ago when they had the chance and nobody wanted it?

It is also well-known to one and all that a grant is payable to modernise such properties as that of which I now wish to speak, and, you may be sure, the character who is selling the property comes into the category of one-and-all, and therefore he knows about the grant, so he sticks that on top of what he reckons the place is worth in order to arrive at the final selling price.

The builder who is called in to carry out the improvements also knows about the grant, and he includes that in his estimate which he submits for doing the job, which he doesn't want anyway, because builders are up to their eyes in work, and it's all the same to him whether you accept his price or not. But he certainly includes the worth of the grant in his estimate.

So what with one thing and another it is quite evident why country people are known by the city types as being quite stupid.

Well, there it is, and here we are, and I wish to tell you about a very nice little property which came on to the market, and the bright young couple came to have a look at it and the old chap showed them round, and the bright young thing of the female gender, which is another way of saying sex, only I didn't want to use the word because of the trouble it can cause, ups and remarks straightaway about the fact that she can't see any water tap and what do they do about that?

So the old chap says it is very silly to have a tap in the house on account of the pipes getting frozen and bursting in the winter and other such awful calamities, but they have a very nice pump in the garden, and the water comes up cool and clear in the summer and no freezing in the winter, and it's a very good idea to have a cupful of water handy by, to prime her first thing in the morning, and a couple of good strokes on the old iron handle and the water don't half come gushing up. So the bright young thing says, 'We can alter that Jeffrey darling, can't we?' and he says, 'Yes, we can alter that, dear.'

So then the bright young thing remarks that she doesn't see any sign of a switch or an electric light about the place, and the old chap explains about the candles they always keep on the shelf over the kitchen door, and discourses on the subject of shorts and fires and rising prices, and the merits of being able to put the candlestick by the side of the bed and put out the candle without having to get out of bed in your bare feet on the cold linoleum just to switch out a light.

So she says, 'We can alter that Jeffrey darling, can't we?' And he says, 'Yes, we can alter that, dear.'

And then they come to the sixty-four thousand dollar question, and the bright young thing remarks about the absence of the certain little room. And the old chap is quite disgusted and says he reckons it's a dirty old habit to do that sort of thing in the house, and folks ought to go outside to do such things, and they've got a proper place for it down in the garden round the corner by the bay tree.

And the door faces east so you can sit there with the morning sun streaming in on you, only keep your foot agin the door in case somebody comes round the corner a bit unexpected like. And the bright young thing goes down to have a look, opens the door, says oh my godfathers, shuts the door quick and comes back to the cottage and says she can see they have a bucket in there.

And the old chap says yes, they have a bucket in there, and good stuff it is, too. Dig it in under the plum tree and you'll get plums as big as your fist, and very juicy at that. The only thing is, he says, not to overdo it. Two years is enough, he says. Then, every third year, dig it in under the rhubarb bed and you'll get rhubarb as thick as your arm.

So the bright young thing says, 'That's all right, but you haven't any bolt on the door.'

And the old chap says oh no, there's no bolt on the door. In fact there's never been a bolt on the door for as long as he can remember. And the bright young thing says, 'But doesn't that worry you?'

And the old chap says, 'No indeed, my dear. There's not a bit of need for you to worry,' he says. 'We've never lost a bucketful in twenty-five years.'

Modern Farmer, Volume 12 Number 7, 1974

Through a plastic glass, darkly

The thought occurred to me at Smithfield Show. Quite where it was, I don't know, and I'm thinking that I should have made a note of it to go back there another year (if there is another year) and try to work out more thoughts on the same basis.

What happened was that I was sitting in this corner and this character gave me a glass of gin and apologised profusely for the fact that the glass was only one of these damned plastic things.

Now when you've studied and observed life for a long time you get to understand about such matters, and I said not to worry because everybody knew it was impossible to find people to do the washing up and, if you don't like it, then go and do it yourself.

Well, I'm not keen on washing up and not much of a hand at it, and I can quite understand the attitude of many other people who don't like washing up any more than I do, with the result that we finish up with everybody using plastic glasses. Instead of washing them you throw them away.

Apart from not being very enthusiastic about washing up, there are many other things I do not think I would do very well, and I was speaking about a great many of them when I was drinking this character's gin, except that he was doing most of the speaking and I was doing most of the listening, which is what makes a good conversationalist.

And because I do not fancy my hand at going down a deep hole in the ground to dig coal, I'd be the last one to stand on a box telling the world what the miners ought to do.

There are also the railway drivers who don't want to

stay away from home overnight, or take the responsibility for too many lives in their hands unless they are paid enough to give them the incentive to stay awake. There are people who don't become over-enthusiastic when you ask them to go down and work in a sewer, those who don't want to wait at table, mix cement, sweep the pavement, deliver post, operate a switchboard and a whole host of subjects it would take pages to fill.

You name it and it's surprising how many people either can't do it or would not want to, or both.

I come into this class on many counts and, come to think of it, I wouldn't want to be called out in the middle of a winter's night and told to put a big leather strap round my waist and climb a pole to see what was the matter and why have the lights gone out.

Oddly enough, all these things have a direct and considerable bearing on the comforts and conveniences of life which we have long since come to take for granted. And if you think about it long enough you see the day rapidly approaching when we shall have to make do without quite a few things in addition to the caviar and the pheasant and the port wine.

In fact, it is not only a question of making do without things, but seeing the whole mighty machine of civilisation grinding to a halt before our very eyes, because we have squandered the resources of the earth and used up all the oil and coal and that, and all we can do is lie down and die and wait for some clever so-and-so's from some other planet to come along millions of years from now and discover all the plastic glasses we threw away, because we didn't know how to get rid of them. And they will still be there, because by the time that happens there will be nobody who likes the job of being a dustman, and I'm in that class as well.

And the plastic glasses will also still be there

because a particular feature of them is that that they're virtually indestructible, which is most useful if you happen to drop one on a stone floor, but can be very embarrassing when the time comes to get rid of them.

So there it is. A thought indeed to make any thinking person miserable beyond words, and I said as much to this character.

So he said to me, if I felt like that, then maybe I shouldn't throw the plastic glass away. So I said, but what could I use it for if I hung on to it?

And he said to hold some more gin. I could drink some more gin couldn't I?

And I said oh, yes, I could do that all right. As long as I didn't have to wash the glasses.

And he said oh, no, we don't wash the glasses because they're plastic and –.

Modern Farmer, Volume 12 Number 9, 1974

Socks

Well there am I at the Royal Show on the Tuesday and the rain is pouring down, so like any other civilised person I take a bit of shelter and the hospitality that goes with it, and a character says to me what about the Indestructible Sock Company, then?

So I say what about it?

And this character says I write a piece about the indestructible plastic glasses, so do I not think that this business of indestructible socks ought to be worth looking into?

The more I think about it the more I think that maybe he has a point and start to wonder whether the socks are indestructible or the company, because it is a fact which is well-known to one and all that Mr Colman once makes his pile on account of all the mustard which people mix up and leave on the plate.

They also reckon that they don't make electric light bulbs to last for ever because they do not wish to go bankrupt.

So in my befuddled state I reason that, if the socks are indestructible, the company cannot be, because people will not go on buying socks and so on and so forth and quod erat demonstrandum.

The more I think about this the more I agree it needs looking into and I come to the conclusion, with it being a show and all that, there must be a bit of a catch in it like non-burn saucepans and one thing and another, and I shudder to think how many such items I have wrapped round my neck in my life when I bring them home.

So when the weather clears I go along to have a look. To my very great surprise I do not find anybody standing up hollering as true as I'm riding this bicycle or dragging a saw across the socks or anything like that. In fact this is a very respectable and tidy outfit altogether, and it seems they are in business since grandfather's day and they just go on from strength to strength. Like the socks in fact.

To start with, the socks have a year's guarantee. Wear them out in that time and you will have them replaced free. But they know of socks that are in action for years and years, so I say well, how do they make a living then?

And they say that after about seventeen years people get fed up with the colour and decide they will like a change, so they throw them away or give them to somebody to wear in their rubber boots.

They are very strong socks but, if you ask me, some socks are such a colour I will not need to wait for seventeen years before I decide I do not like the colour of them. They are diabolical and only a fairy will ever buy socks of such colours.

Now I can see from all this talk that socks which are as strong as these socks are such socks as to be a very good investment and so I buy two pairs of them. One to wear and one to wash.

And I figure that with a bit of luck I need never buy another pair of socks as long as I live, because I do not buy socks of such colours as the fairies wear, so I am not likely to get fed up with the colour and throw them away to litter the place the same as the plastic glasses when people finish drinking their gin.

What is more I need never again have to go round the house hollering for clean socks, because with only two pairs to keep track of you are bound to be sitting in the pound seats.

These socks are also reckoned to be very good on the sweat issue, so what with one thing and another I am very glad I buy two pairs and I will tell you why.

On my return from the show I am dragged off to see a performance of Under Milk Wood, which is written by the so sadly departed and lately-lamented Mr Dylan Thomas.

If I may be permitted to bare my old-fashioned soul to you, let me confess that I think it is nothing but a load of old verbal diarrhoea, but there is no percentage in making such a statement, because it is thought to be very beautiful indeed by all sorts of people, including some of those who wear the same colour socks as the fairies wear.

Maybe it is just that I live too close to the original Llareggub where that particular prophet has very little honour indeed. However, there is a character in this play, or whatever it is supposed to be (I am not yet able to find out) by the name of Polly Garter, who is no better than she ought to be, and she says, 'Nothing ever grows in our garden only washing and babies'.

We will not say anything about the babies on this occasion, but let us confine ourselves to the washing instead. These indestructible socks about which I am telling you are not only indestructible, but have the most effective deodorants known built into them, and it is a fact which is well-known to one and all that there is no more revolting smell in this world than the smell of sweaty socks.

And everybody also knows that the late Mr Thomas is such a character as not to be all that particular whatsoever about changing his socks. And maybe if he ever knows about these indestructible socks with their special deodorants and the chance of getting away with having only two pairs, one to wash and one to wear, he will just stick to the one pair anyway, and maybe he will not write that line about the garden only growing washing.

In fact he may not even write Under Milk Wood at all, which is all about the sort of people who wear sweaty socks. They are certainly not such characters as will throw socks away just because they do not like the colour of them.

And if the late Mr Thomas never writes Under Milk Wood at all I cannot see what loss it will be to an ungrateful nation.

Modern Farmer, April 1975

Dung of praise

A long time ago now – oh, years and years I would say, in fact, even longer than that – Grandad used to have an old book, and there was a poem in it which he used to love reading and the poem used to go like this:

Odes have been writ and praises sung,
*   to almost everything but dung.*
But Oh! what praise is high enough
*   for such rich aromatic stuff?*
See how the mangel-wurzels swell,
*   if you're prepared to do them well.*
See how the wheat springs shoulder high
*   when fed from the stable, byre and sty.*
Look at the barley's drooping ear
*   and dream of mellow dung-fed beer.*
So watch your tumbrels rolling by
*   with naked triumph in your eye.*
For no man spreadeth dung in vain;
*   he giveth to receive again.*

Well, in the end, he grew so old that everybody got fed up with him and said he was just a stupid old goat, because that's what happens when folks grow old, and those of the younger generation always know much better anyway.

Eventually it got that nobody listened to him, and so he upped and died and everybody said what a wonderful old chap he was to be sure, and put on their black shoes and their black ties and looked miserable, especially because the stupid old goat had to go and get himself buried on a dry day when everybody could have been on the land.

And they stuck him away in the corner of the churchyard, and then proceeded to forget all about him and his stupid old poem. And I am bound to admit that it is not such a poem as you will hear being read if you go to a poetry reading where characters wear velvet jackets and big floppy bow ties and sit around looking very soulful about many different matters except dung. They would not look soulful about such a matter as dung, but, if you ask me, that's all some of their poetry is. In fact, it is diabolical.

Anyway, not to make a long story even longer, when Grandad's generation had gone and passed, a new generation came along and really started to get things organised. To start with, they found a much better way of supplying the plant with its food requirements, which was to buy it ready-made-up in bags, and scatter it all over the fields in great profusion, and very quick and effective it was to be sure. And the more of it you put on, the more the grass would grow and the more cows you could keep.

There was only one small problem, and that was that the dung had to be handled, because farmers have better things to do with their time than write poetry and they are not such characters as write poetry to any great extent in any case.

But, as we've said before, cometh the hour cometh the man. And before you could say: 'Where's the demonstration?' there were characters swarming all over the place telling farmers to channel the dung into lagoons, which is what is known as a euphemism, because a lagoon is a very romantic sounding term which is also very evocative of dusky-skinned lulus with plenty of this and that and especially that, with palm trees and coconuts and one thing and another, and the blue seas with surf running up across the golden sands.

But a lagoon is not like that at all. In fact, it is where all the slurry is dumped, and you hope that if you don't look it might go away. So now you know what a euphemism is, because it is nothing but a great big hole in the ground full of a four letter word which is an alternative in the crossword puzzle for dung. It is a most revolting spectacle.

Well, everybody got very excited about the lagoon business and they were so enthusiastic about seeing how fast they could fill them that they soon found themselves in the position where they were buying more fertiliser to grow more grass to keep more cows to produce more milk to get more money to pay for the fertiliser. Until the price of fertiliser hit the ceiling at a hundred smackers a ton and what d'you know about that then Nelly?

So they all put their heads together and decided to have another big demonstration on how valuable this MUCK was and how to handle it to put it on the land. And blow my eyes, to my surprise, when they got to the bottom of the lagoon there was a heap of old junk which some cad had chucked there years ago when nobody was looking and amongst it was a soggy, soiled old book with a poem in it all about dung. So I should think that must be the book Grandad spent his time reading and we wondered what had happened to it.

Modern Farmer, March 1976

Piggy-bank

Well, naturally, I was very interested in the piece in *Modern Farmer* about the vet giving the oil bath and enema to the white rhinoceros, which is why people are awarded such decorations sometimes, although it is not unknown for people to get the OBE for very obscure reasons, and not for anything nearly as meritorious as giving the works to a white rhinoceros.

Furthermore there is much discussion, and there are many hard words being spoken at the moment concerning the RSPCA and their attitude to fox-hunting. Nobody seems to be able to agree on where this organisation should stand on such a delicate and contentious subject. And anybody who thinks it is possible to come up with a quick and easy solution is just as likely to believe that Enoch Powell could come up with an answer to the Irish question.

So what with one thing and another it puts me in mind of the very sad story of the character taking his pig to market in the trailer behind the car with the pig-net over the trailer.

Just as this character is setting off, he pulls out his money to count it, and five one-pound notes drop slap-dab through the pig-netting into the trailer and, before he can make an effective grab for them, the pig has gobbled them up, and hard lines, mate, and what do you know about that?

Anyway, not to make a long story even longer, on his way to market this character calls on the vet, who is by no means in the OBE for white rhinoceros class, but is always willing to do his best, and he offers a box of the very latest pills just on the market. And the treatment is to catch the pig by the snout, flick the pill down his throat, then nip round smartly and give the pig a sharp kick up the enema end.

So this character thinks anything is worth a try and accepts the box of pills and gets the pig to market and unloads him and puts him in a pen to be able to commence the treatment forthwith. Well, the pig must be very surprised to get a kick up the enema end, for, sure enough, he gives a sudden cough and up comes a pound note.

Not surprisingly, there is a dealer watching this performance, because there are always dealers watching everything which goes on in such places, and in all the years he has been keeping his eyes open he never remembers seeing a pig coughing up a pound note, either with or without a kick up the enema end.

And naturally, before anybody else has a chance to see what is going on and get in on such a good thing, he sidles up to this character and says what is this unusual pig, and does he always cough up pound notes, and how much does this character want for him?

Well, you can guess the rest, and the dealer says he wants another demonstration, and then wants to try himself, and each time the pig coughs up a pound note, and before they have finished with him he does not even wait for the kick up the enema end, so who said pigs are stupid?

Then this character reckons up and he knows there are no more pound notes left, so he sticks his toes in, and the dealer says very well he will buy the pig. And although this character knows it is a very ordinary pig, indeed, he now has the dealer in such a fever of excitement that he offers one hundred pounds for the pig and counts them out in fivers, and so the pig is his, and he whips it straight into his truck because it is such a valuable pig. And this character gives him the box with the remainder of the pills just for luck and as a token of good faith.

And that's all there is to the story except that a couple of weeks later this character is sitting by the fire reading the paper, and all of a sudden he starts to laugh, and he says to his wife, 'Well, what d'you think about this then? There's a bloke here just got six months' hard labour for kicking a pig to death.'

And what will the RSPCA have to say about that lot when they have sorted out the business about the fox-hunting?

Mann's Monitor, Winter 1978-1979

Apart from the fact that he hardly knew the difference between a two-thread lug and a slot-side cam brace he reckoned that when it came to ergonomics he knew as much as the next man. All the farming papers had pieces about it, there was a bloke talking about it on the telly and the union organiser had run a course on it. As far as he was concerned it meant comfort when sitting down and convenience to perform the immediate task in hand.

He had learned the basic principles years ago when but a lad, sitting there in the privy out in the garden of a morning with the door open and the warm sun beating in on him. The door opened in.

Even then he had been of an enquiring turn of mind and had noticed that the hinges had been changed round. When he asked his dad, the old chap explained that originally the door had opened out, and what was the use of that. Sitting there all contemplative when, too late to jump up and grab outwards, you'd hear somebody coming. So they moved the hinges for the door to open in, and now all you had to do was sit there with it open and keep your foot against it in readiness.

The old chap had been a ploughman and for hour after hour, day after day, he'd go plodding along behind the horses with his back bent and a sack over his shoulders. But, like the garden privy, those days had gone as well. Ergonomics had changed all that. Nowadays even a tractor was no longer a tractor.

He had discarded his ear muffs because the cab was sound-proofed, and that was just as well because he could listen to the telly as well as watch it. The colour wasn't too good but they had promised to come and see about that. There was no problem about the door to the privy because it was installed *in situ* and the output recycled *en passant*.

Some folks would have said the wall-to-wall carpeting was hardly up to sitting-room standards but it was serviceable and hard-wearing. These were the things which mattered. Let others concern themselves with buttons and electronics and differentials. And there could be no question about it. They knew their job.

This vast new leviathan of a tractor would never wear out and that was for sure. She was never in use for more than one day a week. They had fixed that all right.

Now they were in the Common Market good and proper it was common money, so there was no more arguing about and manipulating the Green Pound. Nowadays it had to be a straight cash deal and they had decided it was necessary to export to survive. And they knew about these things and understood them. So, most of the food was imported, and the new monster tractor was so efficient that in less than one day a week it could, on average, plough enough, sow enough and harvest enough to meet the farm's quota.

And, of course, the factories had to be kept going so they had paid a huge incentive development grant for the farmer to buy the new tractor. And he liked it and was glad of it.

It was almost as if they had foreseen the situation because the bloke living in the tied cottage, which was supposed to have been his, wouldn't get out. So he said if he couldn't have the tied cottage he would adapt his knowledge of ergonomics and make do with the tractor cab as long as they would send the man along please to fix the colour on the telly and any chance of a new carpet?

But, of course, they, the omnipotent and omnipresent they, could not countenance this because of the incentive development grant and what about planning permission anyway, to say nothing of the fact that it could not be permitted under current CAP regulations.

Far more important was the fact that a deputation from the Ministry of Ergonomics was expected any day now to see how the money was being spent and a working demonstration was essential.

Being civil servants they thought they had the answer because the story had come out of Wales the previous summer.

The Welsh Water Authority had a problem. When laying sections of cable ducts they would leave lengths of rope inside the ducts so that, on completion, the rope could be used to pull the cable through. Unfortunately, thieves (possibly English from over the border) began stealing the rope. So now they used Fred, the ergonomic ferret, with a long string tied round its neck to whip through the duct in pursuit of a rabbit skin at the other end. Then the string is used to pull the rope through, and the rope to pull the cable. *Quod erat demonstrandum.*

So, the idea was put forward, and they thought they could adapt it to ferret him out of his ergonomic tractor cab.

But, of course, being civil servants, they didn't know about ferrets and they went and used a polecat ferret. Now practically everybody knows that a polecat places very great store on sense of smell and, when this particular ferret had gone far enough up the duct to get within sniffing distance of the privy *en passant* section of the outfit, some warning bells in his subconscious from way back in his ancestry began to ring out loud and clear. Ergonomic ferret or not he turned back.

The *status quo* has thus been resumed. An impasse has been reached. Professors of ergonomics have a real problem on their hands. And he wants to stress that he has no complaints about the tractor cab whatsoever as long as they send the man to fix the telly. And what about a new carpet?

Notes

Welsh Farm News, **27 June 1959**

For those who know little about the Pembrokeshire islands some brief explanations could be helpful. The more specific references will be found in the books *Cliffs of Freedom, The Sounds Between,* and *Farewell The Islands.*

With the financial support of his father-in-law, the island of Skokholm was rented from the Dale Castle Estate in the 1920s by a Ronald Lockley, who wrote a number of books and articles on his life there. Much of his writing was fanciful, exaggerating his own involvement in numerous events, a fact which was well-known to local people, amongst whom he was something of a joke. As one Marloes wit was heard to say, 'He's a long way from home. A couple of good fields and a burgage.' It was subsequently written of him as being 'a character who had honed and polished to a fine art the ability to extract money by way of grant and subsidy from just about every sort of public fund known to mankind'.

Eventually he formed what he called the West Wales Field Society of which he was Chairman. Initially, when he rented Skokholm, he had conned the RSPB into paying the rent for him. In the late 1950s, when the neighbouring, far more important island of Skomer became vacant, he conned the owner, the Midlands industrialist, Mr Leonard Lee, into selling it to the Nature Conservancy, who put up the money and leased it to Lockley's Society. His behaviour was then so outrageous, and his judgement and management so inept, that leading and well-respected naturalists, at crowded meetings, demanded and obtained his resignation. These meetings were fully reported in the local papers. The Secretary, a Dilwyn Miles, was replaced shortly afterwards.

In 1958 Mr Lee, who had a great affection for Skomer, said in a letter: 'I cannot tell you how sorry I am I sold the island, but I believed I was doing it in the national interest.'

Welsh Farm News, 5 February 1966
It was one thing to have been proved right forty years ago about the likelihood of a hard winter. In the light of the daft talk at that time about the coming of another ice age, it is far more satisfying to be still around to see the other prediction of that time coming true about the current so-called global warming.

Welsh Farm News, 16 December 1967
The outbreak of foot-and-mouth disease in the 1960s was successfully handled, as were previous outbreaks, in a way which puts to shame the disgraceful incompetence of the bureaucrats in failing to deal with the more recent outbreak with its devastating effects in 2001. The incompetence was only compounded when President Blair announced a 'hands-on' approach and that he was taking personal control.

Modern Farmer, April 1975
As will be noted, these lines were penned more than sixty years ago, but the saying is that man changes but little.